Repayable

Repayable

Student Loan Debt Solutions For Your Financial Freedom

Jeni Burckart

ISBN: 1539910903
ISBN 13: 9781539910909
Library of Congress Control Number: 2016918595
CreateSpace Independent Publishing Platform
North Charleston, South Carolina

Dedication

This book is dedicated to everyone with student loan debt. You bettered yourself through education and recognize the burden of student loan debt like no one else. Let this book serve as a light in the financial darkness.

Contents

Acknowledgments · · · · · · · · · · · · · ix

Introduction · · · · · · · · · · · · · · · · xi

Chapter 1   An Exposé of Student Loan Debt · · · 1
Chapter 2   How Much is Too Much? · · · · · · · · 25
Chapter 3   Ways to Repay · · · · · · · · · · · · · · 43
Chapter 4   Reconsider Your Rates · · · · · · · · · · 65
Chapter 5   Please Forgive Them · · · · · · · · · · · 85
Chapter 6   The Democracy of Debt · · · · · · · · 107
Chapter 7   Reliable Sources · · · · · · · · · · · · · 129
Chapter 8   Dominate Your Debt · · · · · · · · · · 143
Chapter 9   A New Hope · · · · · · · · · · · · · · · 165
Chapter 10   Make it Viral · · · · · · · · · · · · · · · 185

Bibliography · · · · · · · · · · · · · · · · · 201
About the Author · · · · · · · · · · · · · 207

Acknowledgments

I would like to thank my parents, Pat and Ann, for raising me with confidence to solve problems and create change. Because of your conviction —that one person can make a difference— I look for solutions and relentlessly push for the transformation I see possible.

I appreciate the perspective my siblings, Kim and Mike, give me. You help me see the world outside myself and rarely let me take an extreme perspective unchallenged. Thank you for being honest, open, and supportive.

Thank you to Eric for your encouragement and belief in my ability to work through problems, find solutions, and spread the word.

Thank you to all my friends who inspired me to write this book. College cost you and the burden of student loan debt is heavy. I'm not leaving the solutions up to anyone else. With a world full of innovative millennials we will find solutions to relieve that burden.

Introduction

You went to college for the experience, education, and future it promised. The cost of your education continued to rise as you pursued your degree. If you're lucky you got scholarships or grants to alleviate some of the need for student loans. Despite your best efforts, by the time you graduated you had a small fortune tied up in student loan debt.

For the first time in years there's a generation of young adults saddled with debt with no commodity to sell. Your parent's generation graduated college (if they went) and had little debt. Their first big purchase was a car or home. They started their adult lives financially free. Not so for us.

It feels like the only ones who care about the massive burden of student loan debt are those of us being crumpled by it. Unfortunately we are some of the least financially influential individuals and get little pull in Congress. We're also some of the least financially experienced, making the student loan debt burden doubly damaging.

Your situation demands a solution. It's up to you and to me, those battling through student loan debt, to develop solutions. We are the people afflicted by student loan debt and the only ones motivated enough to save future generations from the fate of never-ending tuition hikes and sky-high interest rates.

It's up to you to arm yourself with the facts and understand the reasonable financial limits of an education.

You can make the best financial decision by choosing the best repayment plan, refinancing to a lower interest rate, or finding a loan forgiveness option.

Repayable highlights how current legislation impacts student loan debt and familiarizes you with the best resources for student loan debt information so you can join in pushing for change.

Once you're finished with *Repayable* you will be empowered by your role in repayment, thinking about possibilities for the future, and accustomed to talking about your debt.

My voice alone isn't enough to be the driving force for change. Hundreds of us won't make the difference either. We need thousands of voices joined together to innovate the changes we need.

Change begins by talking to your fellow indebted comrades honestly. Then conversation expands to discussing your debt burden with the folks who don't relate to student loan debt. Eventually it becomes part of the discussion when negotiating compensation with a potential employer. In time it reaches the top and legislative changes bring widespread relief.

I wrote this book while actively repaying my own six-figure debt because I know your student loan debt struggle. I understand that repayment is about more than sheer determination and financial sacrifice. It's about finding the best way for you to repay your debt without social deprivation and a life eating ramen noodles.

I recognize that change is often brought about by those who need it most. Thankfully our millennial generation is resourceful, innovative, and relentless. These attributes will serve you well in your quest to make your student loans repayable.

For college-educated millennials, balancing student loan payments with the cost of young adult life is harder than ever. You can't make big life decisions like buying a home without giving serious thought to your student loan debt.

Repayable is the book that clearly explains ways to repay your student loans without sacrificing the quality of life you earned through higher-education.

Repayable is designed to clear up the mystery surrounding student loan debt. There is no "one size fits all" method for student loan repayment. This book concisely explains options from repayment plans and refinancing to loan forgiveness. *Repayable* is for anyone who feels trapped by their student loans and unable to see the end of their repayment.

As a millennial who graduated with $132,000 in student loan debt, I've tried everything to knock my debt down. In two years I've managed to repay over $45,000 in principle while still being able to do things I love like travel to NYC, the Grand Canyon, and Alaska.

Whether your student loan debt is large or small, you will find a strategy in this book that minimizes the sting of student loan repayment and lets you live your life.

I promise that when you read through the clear explanations of your repayment options you will find a better way to repay your student loans while maintaining or even improving your lifestyle. AND I promise you will be fired up to create bigger change for everyone with student loan debt so no one lets their debt get in the way of living life.

Don't be the person who puts their entire life on hold to repay their student loans. Be the person who tackles their debt while enjoying the experiences that mean the most. Make people wonder how you manage to get so much out of your finances. Be someone who takes charge of their financial life and does it now.

The student loan repayment strategies you're about to read can be applied to your unique loan situation. All you have to do to alleviate the crippling effects of your student loan debt is keep reading. Each chapter will give you new information you can apply to ease the burden of student loan debt and create a better outcome for current and future college graduates.

Take control of your student loan debt right now, make the most of your money, and enjoy life while making your loans truly repayable.

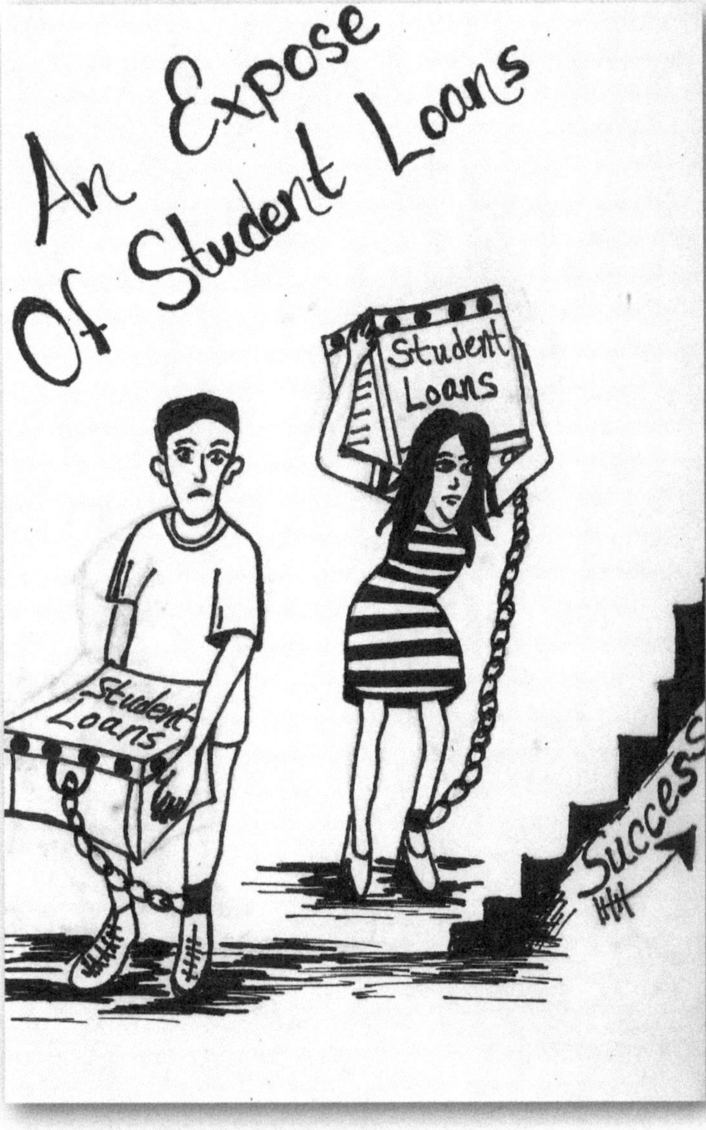

Chapter 1

An Exposé of Student Loan Debt

There's a lot of information swirling about in the media when it comes to the millennial generation. Financial stats abound and the information looks bleak.

What have I gotten myself into? You've likely wondered more than once as you glance at your Department of Education balance.

The key to conquering any enemy is to understand it. This chapter will serve as a bit of kindling to light the fires of change.

This chapter is data-driven and intense. You might feel overwhelmed with numerical information. It's ok to take a break and go on to another chapter. It's ok to peace out and read the rest of the book. You come back when you think of a question, the facts aren't going anywhere.

After reading this chapter you'll have an objective, data-driven chunk of information to shut down the naysayers and critics who refuse to address student loan debt. Willful ignorance has done nothing to reduce your interest rates or stop year after year of increasing tuition.

It's time that the biggest financial burden of the largest living generation is addressed. If no one else can understand and address student loan debt, those living it need to be empowered to develop their own solutions.

This exposé addresses the average debt of recent graduates, the increase in tuition over time and changing interest rates. These data are compared to historic counterparts and adjusted for inflation to provide a benchmark for meaningful evaluation.

By looking at multiple points in time we can identify trends and look for causes.

If we're going to build a movement, we will build a rock solid, objective, data-driven movement. A movement built on facts so we can shut critics down with the truth and provoke an era of repayable higher education.

Why do we need to build a fact-based case for the burden of student loan debt?

Because our generation needs to bring about acceptance that student loan debt is a financial burden that impacts society at large.

I want you to be able to defend your financial situation to those who criticize millennials as "entitled". I want you to provide smart counsel to your younger siblings and friends who aren't sure what to do about financing their education. I want you to be able to debate folks who think student loan debt is no big deal with facts and stats.

You can shape the future by developing ideas for improvement of the current student loan debt situation.

You will do all this by having a thorough understanding of the history and current state of student loans.

It's time to uncover the dirt, roll up those sleeves, and read on.

Total Cost of College Attendance Over Time

You've heard it before. College tuition is rising incredibly fast, faster than other costs, and faster than wages. So is it true? Or is it just propaganda?

Let's find out.

According to the National Center for Education Statistics (NCES) the 2014-2015 cost for tuition & fees plus room and board for all institutions has increased by 2.25 times the 1963-1964 amount.[1]

Well, you might be thinking to yourself, *the overall cost of living has decreased and so things even themselves out.* No, the first statistic demonstrates a total increase which includes room & board.

Have room and board indeed decreased rather than increased over time?

Have room and board remained the same while tuition has been the primary contributor to cost of attendance increases?

Let's examine the facts.

**All values below are reported in constant 2014-2015 dollars to allow you to make a straightforward comparison.

---

1 NCES Table 330.10. Average undergraduate tuition and fees and room and board rates charged for full-time students in degree-granting postsecondary institutions, by level and control of institution: 1963-64 through 2014-15

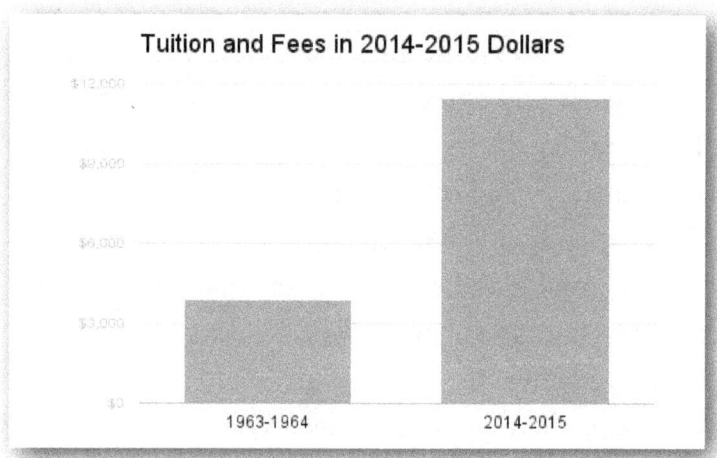

Average cost of tuition & fees for all institutions in 1963-1964 was $3,900 in 2014-2015 it was $11,487[2]. That's a 2.95-fold increase!!! Essentially tuition and fees cost three times the amount today as they did in 1963.

So what about room and board?

In 1963-1964 the price for a dorm room was $2,167 in 2014-2015 it was $5,719[3]. An increase of 2.64 times the 1963-1964 amount

---

2 NCES Table 330.10 Average tuition and required fees, all institutions.
3 NCES Table 330.10 Dormitory rooms, all institutions.

In 1963-1964 the price of board (see footnote[4]) was \$3,510 and the cost in 2014-2015 was \$4,523.[5] This is by far the lowest increment of increase at only 1.29 times the old school amount.

Why split out the different statistics like this?

Because I have heard critics say that living expenses have gone down so tuition increases look bad but in reality aren't.

Welp, there goes that idea, looks like *everything* has continued to get more expensive over time although tuition demonstrates the largest increases.

Perhaps the data looks so bad because we're looking at all colleges.

Public institutions are known to be less expensive so the cost of attendance will be skewed if we include private colleges rather than looking only at public institutions.

---

4 Data for 1986-87 and later years reflect a basis of 20 meals per week, while data for earlier years are for meals served 7 days a week (the number of meals per day was not specified). Because of this revision in data collection and tabulation procedures, data are not entirely comparable with figures for previous years. In particular, data on board rates are somewhat higher than in earlier years because they reflect the basis of 20 meals per week rather than meals served 7 days a week. Since many institutions serve fewer than 3 meals each day, the 1986-87 and later data reflect a more accurate accounting of total board costs.

5 NCES Table 330.10 Board, all institutions.

Reminding you that unbelievably all these comparisons are made in constant 2014-2015 dollars AKA inflation-adjusted.

In 1963-1964 the cost of attending a 4 year public institution was $7,126 in 2014-2015 it was $18,632[6] which represents a 2.6 fold increase in cost of attendance and mirrors the data for all colleges.

Let's take a look at just tuition and fees without room and board.

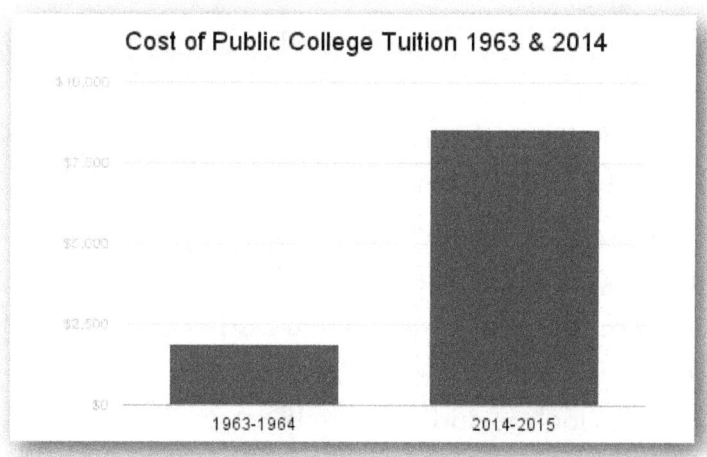

In 1963-1964 tuition and fees at 4 year public institutions was $1,867 and in 2014-2015 it was

---

6 NCES Table 330.10 Cost of attendance, 4-year public institutions

$8,543.[7] This means **the cost of tuition more than quadrupled at 4-year public institutions!**

And *still* people insist that college is affordable for you because it was for them. Many demand that if you just worked hard enough you could pay for college yourself without borrowing money. The facts just don't add up to that possibility.

If public institutions had such a disproportional increase in tuition then maybe private institutions are the way to go.

Did private institutions exhibit a smaller degree of change in tuition?

In 1963-1964 tuition at 4-year private nonprofit and for-profit institutions the average cost of attendance was $13,887 and in 2014-2015 it was $42,065[8]. That's a 3.03 fold increase, which is slightly above the increase found in 4-year public institutions (2.6 fold increase).

Let's look at tuition by itself.

---

7 NCES <u>Table 330.10</u> Tuition and fees, 4-year public institutions

8 NCES <u>Table 330.10</u> Cost of attendance, 4-year private nonprofit and for-profit institutions

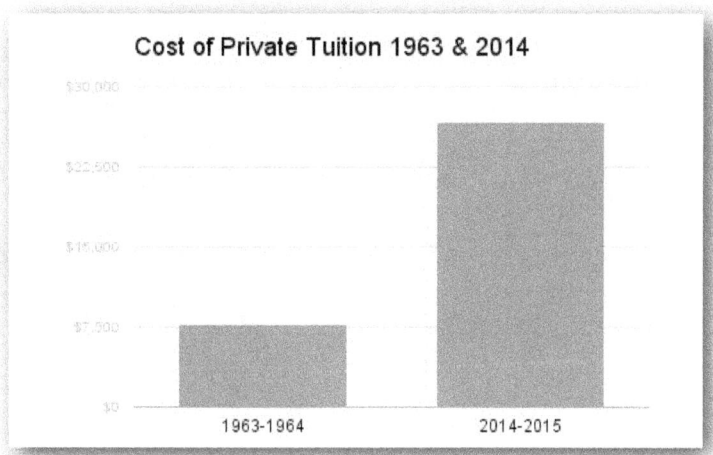

Cost of Private Tuition 1963 & 2014

In 1963-1964 tuition and fees at 4-year private nonprofit and for-profit institutions cost $7,757 and in 2014-2015 cost $26,740[9] an increase of 3.45 times.

These data demonstrate that private institutions had a smaller proportional increase in tuition and fees than public institutions. However, the cost of tuition and fees at a private institute is still higher than at a public institution.

Let's compare the 2014-2015 numbers.

---

9 NCES Table 330.10 tuition and fees, 4-year private nonprofit and for-profit institutions

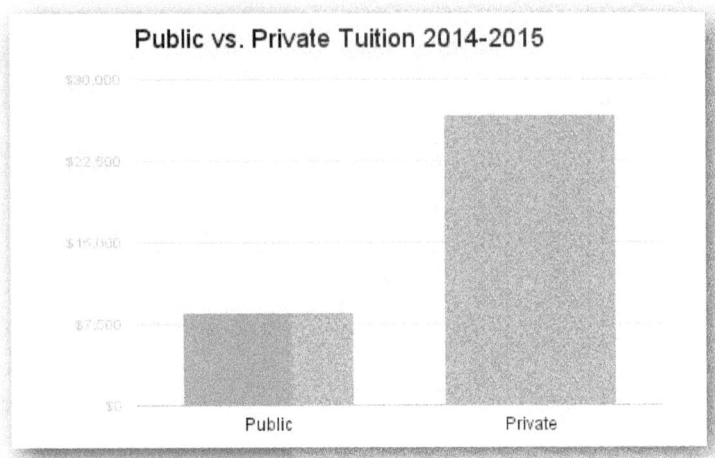

Public vs. Private Tuition 2014-2015

Cost of tuition and fees at a 4-year public institution in 2014-2015 was $8,543[7] and the cost for a nonprofit or for profit private 4-year institution was $26,740[9].

So in the end, the average private institution costs $18,197 more than average public institution. Over four years that ends up being $72,788.

Changes in Student Loan Debt Over Time

So maybe the cost to attend college has gone up. But there are tons of Pell grants, scholarships, and other sources of funding. So that means the actual amount the student ends up spending is less.

Let's find out.

The data for debt information is from another source. This information is based on calculations by The Institute for College Access & Success (TICAS). TICAS obtained their data from the U.S. Department of Education, National Center for Education Statistics, Integrated Postsecondary Education Data System (IPEDS) and Peterson's Undergraduate Financial Aid and Undergraduate Databases, (copyright 2015 Peterson's, a Nelnet company, all rights reserved).

These data are reported by individual states and I'm not able to feature all 50 states. For the sake of transparency and highest level of applicability if your state isn't featured check out http://ticas.org/posd/map-state-data-2015 to find state's debt information. I will be featuring a few select states; Wyoming, Alaska, Virginia, Washington, Iowa, and Wisconsin.

I will look at Iowa and Wisconsin because I've lived in both these places and want to examine the state of student loan debt in my home territories.

The remaining states had the highest quality data reporting of graduates' debt information (>90% of graduates were represented in the usable data).

Wyoming had the very best and reported 100% of graduates both years.

All six of these states data have a strong robustness score which means at least two-thirds of data came from colleges that reported student debt data in both years.

The data available unfortunately doesn't span as many years as the NCES data. The data TICAS provides is the 10-year change in student loan debt. This means we'll be comparing 2004 to 2014 numbers.

Please take note that the reported numbers are not adjusted for inflation ($1 in 2004 = $1.25 in 2014) but the visual comparison chart is adjusted for inflation.

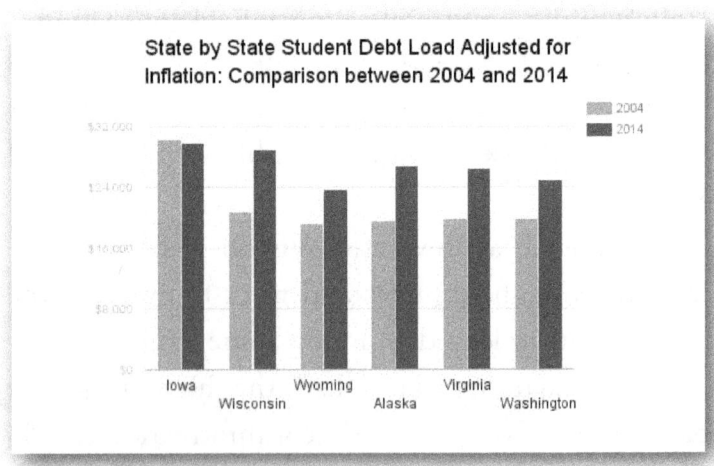

Let's start with my home state of Iowa.

In 2004 76% of graduates earned their degree with debt. The average debt was $24,204 while in 2014 68% of graduates earned their degree with debt (that percentage went down?!) and the average debt was $29,732. If this is adjusted for inflation there is almost no change in the value of the debt these students graduated with and it appears to have decreased by $500.

Why did the percentage of students graduating with debt and the total debt amount decrease over those 10 years? It's difficult to say but I suspect a significant reporting bias here.

In 2004 only 74% of graduates were represented in the usable data but in 2014 94% of graduates were captured. Perhaps of those graduates represented in the 2004 data the graduates reported came from private institutions, professional degrees, or graduate programs. All of these scenarios would have higher costs and could shift the data.

Overall the Iowa data does not fit the trend of the rest of the states listed here with better reporting.

Let's take a look at Wisconsin.

In 2004 60% of graduates finished with debt. The average debt was \$16,560. While in 2014 70% of graduates finished with debt and the average debt load was \$28,810. When adjusted for inflation this an increase of about \$8,000 in ten years.

Unfortunately Wisconsin may also be subject to a little reporting bias. In 2004 only 77% of graduates were represented in usable data compared to 89% represented in 2014.

So let's look at a state where 100% of graduates were captured both years.

Let's examine the information on debt from Wyoming.

In 2004 44% of graduates exited with student loan debt. The average amount of debt was \$15,352. In 2014 46% of graduates finished with debt and the average debt was \$23,708. When adjusted for inflation this is an increase of about \$4500.

Let's look at data from three other states with >90% reporting in both years, Alaska, Virginia, and Washington.

We'll start with Alaska.

In 2004 48% of graduates finished with student loan debt. The average debt was \$15,648. In 2014

50% of graduates finished with an average student loan debt of $26,742. When adjusted for inflation that's just over a $7,000 increase in total debt over ten years.

Let verify the debt situation in Virginia.

In 2004 57% of graduates finished college with an average of $15,831 in student loan debt. In 2014 60% of graduates finished with an average of $26,432 in student loan debt. When adjusted for inflation this represents an increase of about $6,600 in debt load over ten years.

Finally let's finish up with Washington state.

In 2004 56% of Washington graduates finished college with an average of $17,415 in student loan debt. In 2014 58% of Washington graduates finished college with an average of $24,804 in student loan debt. When adjusted for inflation that represents an increase of about $3,000 in total student loan debt over ten years.

So of the six states examined five had more students graduating with even higher amounts of debt in 2014 compared to 2004. The one state that didn't demonstrate an increase (Iowa) may have demonstrated a selection bias in previous reporting.

This information demonstrates that scholarships and grant money are not keeping up with the cost of attending college.

If scholarship and grant money kept up with cost of attendance increases the average amount and number of students graduating with debt would either stay the same or decrease.

Change in Interest Rates Over Time

One of the biggest challenges facing student loan borrowers is the staggering interest rates. Interest rates for car and home loans are often lower than the interest rates of federally funded loans.

Student loan interest rates reflect the market interest rates.

Below you'll find a table comparing interest rates for the top two sources of consumer debt in America; student loan debt and mortgages.

But Jeni, interest rates are credit-dependent- how can you make an accurate comparison?

For each example I will assume an average credit score of 638 which is based on data compiled by Credit

Karma for the average score of 18-24 year olds. This is prime college-age so the comparison is logical. Interest rates for student loans don't depend on credit scores.

Table 1 Interest rates for federal student loans and mortgages *(Federal Student Aid an Office of the Department of Education, 2016) (Federal Reserve, 2015)* https://www.statburcau.org/en/united-states/inflation-tables

Year	2006	2008	2010	2012	2015
Federal Student Loan Interest Rate (%)	5.3	6.8	5.6 (S) 6.8 (US)	3.4 (S) 6.8 (US)	4.29 (S) 6.8 (US)
Mortgage Interest Rate (%)	3.66	4.69	6.04	6.41	3.85
Year over Year Inflation (%)	2.54	0.09	1.5	1.74	0.73

An interesting thing I picked out from the table is that subsidized loan interest rates seem to correlate better with mortgage rates and inflation. However, the interest rates for unsubsidized loans don't change in respect to current interest rates.

I find this a curious trend. The amount of money a college student can borrow in subsidized loans is limited to $3,500 the first year, $4,500 the second year, $5,500 the third year and beyond. Graduate and professional students aren't eligible to borrow subsidized loans.

The total amount of subsidized loans that could be taken out during four years of college is $19,000[10] which is well below the expected cost of attendance and below the average amount of debt students graduate with.

Why is this such a big deal? It means students are forced to borrow additional money that accrues interest while they're pursuing their education. It also means their unsubsidized federal loans have less competitive interest rates. So these students are being hit twice by interest rates.

---

10 https://studentaid.ed.gov/sa/types/loans/subsidized-unsubsidized#how-much

Types of Available Employment and Salary Based on Education Level

*The following statistics are obtained from the bureau of labor statistics 2013 data. http://www.bls.gov/careeroutlook/2014/article/education-level-and-jobs.htm

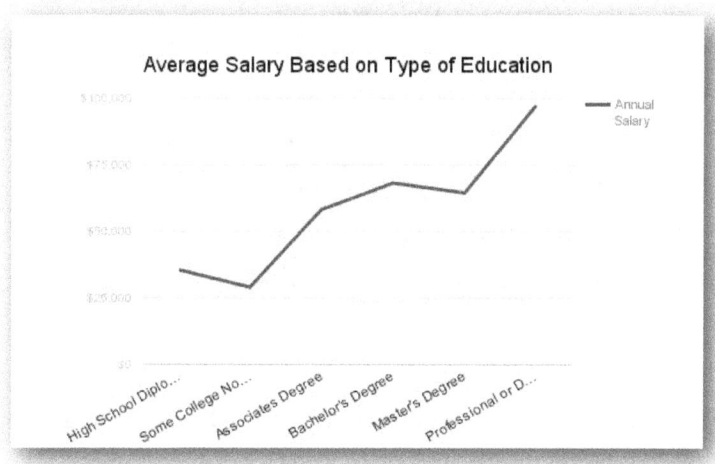

In the US 38.9 % of employment requires only a high school diploma. The median annual wage for jobs that require only a high school diploma is $35,580.

An additional 11.6% of employment requires some college, a post-secondary non-degree award, or an associate's degree. The median annual wage ranges from $29,100 (for some college with no degree) to $58,240 (for associate's degree).

In the US 18 % of available employment requires a bachelor's degree. That bachelor's degree will earn you a median annual wage of $68,180.

Employment requiring a master's degree makes up 1.7% of jobs. Unfortunately the median annual wage is $64,510.

That should make you scratch your head and think carefully. A higher level of education (a master's degree), requiring two years of lost wages, and an additional two years of tuition, actually has a lower median annual wage than just a bachelor's degree.

The key lesson in this finding is that more education does not automatically equal more money.

In the US 2.6% of occupations require a professional or doctoral degree. The average annual wage is $97,550.

So what are the lessons this information is trying to show you? I'll get into the best and worst degrees from a financial perspective in more detail in the very next chapter. As you move into that chapter keep the following in mind.

* Obtaining some college education without a certificate or degree is a financial nightmare. It leads to debt without an increase in pay.
* **More education ≠ more money.**

Knowledge is Power

You've consumed a chapter filled with stats regarding everything from tuition costs over time, to inflation information, to changes in interest rates, to types of employment available across the country.

But Jeni, these statistics paint a grim picture, you used the most extreme statistics.

These statistics represent the average, and the sources are transparent. If there's something you're questioning I encourage you to research it further.

Ultimately, when using statistics that are averages there are always outliers who are better or worse off than the average demonstrates.

What are you going to do with all this newfound knowledge?

Use it to spread the word. It's your responsibility to share this information so we have a country full of people on the same page. It's difficult to bring about change to fix a problem that a large percent of the population doesn't feel the consequences of.

There are people out there who think that college is no more expensive today than it was in the past. You now have a chapter's worth of data contradicting that.

There are people who think that although tuition has gotten more expensive financial aid has gotten better, so the amount of money a student actually pays has gone down. You now have data demonstrating that's not the case.

Some folks may believe that while college is expensive and graduates carry a considerable amount of debt, the types of jobs college graduates get make up for the increased costs.

This belief is sometimes valid and sometimes not and requires a deeper dive to fully examine. The truth is that for some types of degrees the financial gain is apparent while for other types of degrees you can dig yourself into a financial hole.

Well Jeni, facts are nice but what am I supposed to do with this information?

The entire rest of this book will get into the action phase. Your only action step for this chapter is to share an interesting fact you learned with someone else face to face or via social media. Go to www.repayable.org/facts to find tweetable, shareable facts.

Chapter 2

How Much is Too Much?

"**G**o to college." or "Get a degree." is given out to high school students as if it were the single most important piece of advice of their lives. Unfortunately that advice is rarely followed up with any further direction.

The unspoken question is, does going to college and getting any degree at any cost get you ahead in life?

This chapter is here to tell you that financially, no. Sometimes going to college just to go is a financially terrible idea and can leave you in a financial mess.

This chapter isn't here to debate the philosophical, educational, or personal merit of a college degree. It's purely a financial assessment.

You need to be deliberate with your college education. College isn't a zero sum game where you can just get any type of education, perform well or poorly, and land a job that will repay your debt.

This chapter will help you understand how to decide if the price tag of your college degree financially matches your expected increase in income.

It's important to know if your degree will lead to the type of job that pays for the lifestyle you're trying to achieve rather than only being able to afford paying your student loans. This chapter will help you identify that.

At some point after graduation, maybe early on, everyone wonders if they should get additional education.

Is a master's degree in my field worth it? Should I sacrifice two years of income and my life to get more education?

As demonstrated in the previous chapter more school ≠ more money.

If you haven't gotten your college degree or you're on the fence about going back for more education this chapter will help you decide what level of education will actually help you start making money and living the lifestyle you wanted your education to provide you.

Financially, it's important to avoid getting into debt to earn the same amount of money you could without a degree.

To help you make the smartest financial choice this chapter identifies some of the best and worst paying degrees and explain the debt:income ratio so you can make informed and objective decisions that make education an investment that repays you for your sacrifice.

But Jeni the value of education isn't tied solely into its financial footprint. Just because my chosen degree doesn't pay for itself doesn't mean it isn't worth it.

I'm not arguing about the merit of a college education. After all, I went to six years of college to earn my Pharm.D. I've experienced firsthand the personal growth that comes from getting a college education. I've also experienced firsthand the reality of paying back $132,000 in student loan debt. Plain and simple if I wasn't a pharmacist I would never be able to afford to repay that loan amount.

Being buried under student loan debt that you can't afford to pay limits your other options in life. Career is only one aspect of your life and the cost of that career can bleed into your relationships and steal away some of your happiness.

I strongly caution a degree choice that doesn't repay unless you have a financial path (like scholarship money or a college fund) that enables you to avoid this sort of upside down debt.

There are so many different degrees, sometimes a shift within the same field can lead to a degree that has a better debt:income ratio, sometimes getting the degree at a different college can shift that ratio in your favor. If you don't look for it to make financial sense you won't save yourself financial headache in the future. You don't have to sell your soul to get a job that pays back your debt.

Debt:Income; the Leveler of Majors

It seems that choosing a major is an impossible task.

How can anyone know what major is best for them?

There are countless choices.

When you compare majors based on financial merit some objectivity appears to help you choose.

The best way to do this is to calculate the expected debt:income ratio. The goal of the debt:income ratio is to serve as an objective marker of the financial discomfort required to repay your debt. The higher the debt:income ratio the more difficult it will be for you to repay your debt.

So how do you figure out your debt:income ratio?

First you need to estimate the total debt you will graduate with, including any interest that accrues on unsubsidized loans while you're in college. To estimate your total debt at graduation take your current annual tuition and multiply it by the number of years you plan to attend college.

For a more conservative estimate increase tuition by 5% annually. So if year one costs you $1,000 —yea right— year two will cost $1,050, year three will cost $1,102, and year four will cost $1,258. So your total debt after four years will be $4,410 rather than $4,000.

Now that you have your debt estimate it's time to estimate income.

Decide on a few of the jobs that are available after you graduate with your planned major. You should pick job titles that you are actually considering, not job titles that pay well but you don't intend to pursue.

Go to payscale.com or another similar website and enter the information needed to estimate a starting salary. Keep track of these numbers.

Are there significant differences in pay between your jobs of interest?

Your final step is to divide your debt by your estimated income. Ideally, this ratio shouldn't be more than 1:1 or 1.5:1.

The higher your expected income the higher tolerance you will have for debt. When you make $100k vs. $50k you have more money available after paying for basic costs of living (food, utilities, rent, etc.). That means you will be able to pay a larger percent of your income toward debt without feeling the same impact as someone who makes less money.

The lower your annual estimated income the lower you want that debt:income ratio to be.

Use this debt:income strategy as an objective tool to help you decide between majors.

Degrees That Cost More Than Their Pay Increase

Not all degrees and majors are created equally. There are some programs of study that lead to a negative financial return on investment.

These majors take time, sacrifice, and money to earn just like all the rest. The problem is that they have high rates of unemployment and low starting salaries. Some majors have average wages comparable to employment that doesn't require any college education.

That means you will pay to go to college for four years, sacrifice four years of full-time income, and sacrifice your time to get an education without actually seeing a financial return. Oh, and you will still need to repay that debt, every month, with no additional pay from your degree to do it.

I think most of you reading this book would prefer to avoid a financial end game like that.

I'm going to explore in depth an example of a degree that doesn't pay.

I will provide an estimate of the annual starting salary compared to the average annual wage of someone without any college education and an estimate of the 10 year student loan payments on the max amount of subsidized loans you can borrow in four years..

Remember these are all averages and I expect people to fall both above and below these estimates.

This solely a financial comparison. In no way am I demeaning the merit of the the degree, the value it adds to our society, or the decision-making skills of someone who chooses to pursue this degree. The following comparison takes into account only salary and doesn't account for benefits like healthcare, retirement, and time off.

Early childhood education: average starting salary $30,300 and mid-career average salary of $38,000. Let's compare that to the average median annual income for high school graduates of $35,580.

Yikes, that means you paid to get an education and now make less than the median annual salary for folks with only a high school diploma.

For a conservative debt estimate let's say you took out only subsidized loans in the four years required to get your degree. Leaving you with a debt load of $19,000.

For a 10 year repayment plan you would pay $200/month. The variety of income-based repayment plans give you payments of $104/month to $200/month with varying periods of repayment.

That means starting out of the gate you will make $440 less per month, plus you will have to pay $200 per month on your student loans, plus you sacrificed four years of full-time income.

Over the course of 10 years you will have $76,800 less than someone who never attended college. That's not counting the four years of lost income while attending college.

This is how student loan debt ends up "upside down". Financially you are worse off for attending college than if you had never gone to college.

You're probably thinking to yourself right about now *but Jeni what about the other 30 years of a career?*

Good question, let's compare the mid-career average salary to the national average for high school graduates.

By the middle of your early childhood education career you will make $202 more per month than someone with only a high school degree. That's $72,720 more dollars earned over 30 years.

If you're looking closely at the numbers you probably have a sick feeling in your gut. Yep, even over the course of 40 years you will still be behind financially by about $4,000.

That's not to say there isn't merit in obtaining a degree to do a specific kind of work with a particular population. This is purely a financial comparison. If you get scholarships and have less debt your financial picture might change.

Completing Some College Without Obtaining a Degree or Certification

Debt without added income is disastrous, as the early childhood education example showed. The problem with some college without a degree is that you didn't give yourself the opportunity to make more income at any point down the road.

In that case you will have debt but you won't have any additional income to help recoup the costs of that education, or the income lost while obtaining it.

So what should you do if you've started but haven't finished a degree?

Figure out how far away from that degree you are (i.e. how many credit hours do you still need). Identify what stopped you from obtaining the degree the first time, is that barrier still there? Decide if you will continue working or go back to school full-time. Determine the cost of tuition and the financial loss if you decide to stop working.

Now figure out your expected salary upon graduation and your expected debt. Compare your expected salary with a degree to your current salary with no change. Multiply the difference by the number of years you expect to work and subtract your monthly student loan payments.

Are you financially ahead if you finish your degree? If so, go for it. If you're not but you still really want to finish your degree, do your best to obtain scholarship or grant money and work as much as possible to minimize your college costs.

Borrow only what you absolutely need to borrow for tuition and books. Anything you can pay for yourself saves you financial headache in the future.

Private vs. Public Colleges

Not all colleges are created equal when it comes to the amount they charge to obtain a degree. Let me show you the most recent (2013-2014) total annual cost of attendance for private four year institutions vs. public four year institutions.[11]

Annual Cost of Attendance at Private 4-year Institution : $36,589.

Annual Cost of Attendance at Public 4-year Insitution: $18,110

Over the course of four years the cost at a private college exceeds the cost of a public college by $73,916.

There is more than just the cost of tuition that factors into the expense of a private college. Many private colleges offer better scholarships and more financial aid than public institutions. That means that the actual debt you would accrue by attending a private college could be less than a public institution.

If you're considering attending a private institution find out what you could expect to receive in financial aid. Many colleges will provide estimates of

---

11 https://nces.ed.gov/fastfacts/display.asp?id=76

what the average student receives as part of their financial aid package.

However without additional scholarships the cost to attend a public institution is considerably lower.

You should strongly consider a public institution as a way to save yourself thousands of dollars in student loan debt.

Most public universities have excellent rankings (better than private institutions) for many fields of study. This is because big universities attract grant money and researchers. If you're in the Midwest, you are particularly lucky because our states are known for their excellent quality public education.

In-state vs. Out-of-state Tuition

Another way to save yourself some student loan debt is to attend a college in your home state, or attend in a state that has reciprocity with your state.

In-state vs. out-of-state tuition differs by thousands of dollars, with out-of-state tuition being more expensive. The idea is that at a public institution the state doesn't get funding for non-residents to attend so they pass the lost subsidy provided by the state onto the student.

If you have decent colleges in your home state I strongly encourage you to attend them. You will pay much less for a similar quality education.

College rankings matter when you're comparing a program that's ranked 100 compared to number 1 but don't matter so much when you're already comparing high-quality programs.

What if I already have a "worthless" degree?

Well Jeni, this advice is great and all but it's too little too late for me. I already have mountains of student loan debt with not much income to repay it.

If you're already feeling the burden of a debt load that's too high for your income, fear not. There's advice for you. The advice isn't going to be easy, there's no "out" for you, but there are strategies to minimize the financial distress and give you a solid plan for repayment.

Your first option that requires the least amount of effort on your part is to set up an income-based repayment plan. This plan will allow you to avoid defaulting on your loans without restricting your cash flow so badly that you can't breathe.

The next options involve some effort on your part and a mindset shift.

You can become an entrepreneur. You have an issue of too little money, so make more of it. So maybe you don't have any desire to be an entrepreneur. You can consider changing fields. Figure out the skills you built with your degree and think of creative ways to use them. A lot of the skills built in a program can transfer well to other disciplines.

If there's not a license or certification required look for jobs in better-paying fields.

Don't want to change fields? Build other skills that can help you take better paying work within your field. Consider taking an online course through The Great Courses or Lynda to learn skills for relatively cheap.

If you can do something that no one else can, you may be a more attractive employee who's worth paying a little bit more. Or worst case scenario you might have a new skill you can hire out as a freelancer on a website like Upwork.

If none of these options appeal to you and you work in certain fields you may be eligible for loan forgiveness. If you work at a non-profit organization for 10 years (and make 120 income-based repayments) the remaining balance of your federal loans may be able to be forgiven at the end of 10 years.

Otherwise with the income-based repayment plan the remainder of your federal student loan debt after making payments for 20 years may be forgiven. The forgiven amount is taxable.

Jeni all this financial talk is fine, but I just really want a particular degree and I don't care about the money.

Ask yourself why you want the degree.

What do you picture your life to be like when you have that specific degree?

Now factor in your student loan payments.

Can you still live the lifestyle you originally envisioned?

If so go after it! If not, consider other better-paying options or adjusting your lifestyle expectations.

This chapter may have painted a difficult financial picture of the cost of college. Unfortunately, without a change in the way education is funded in the US you must consider the financial impact your degree will have on your lifestyle.

I may have cited in detail one particularly drastic and bleak example of upside down debt. Remember, the national average annual income for folks with a bachelor's degree is still much higher than for folks with a high school diploma.

The current advice already tells you to "go to college" because "you will earn more money". The goal of this chapter is to help you make an educated decision so you actually do make more money.

I don't want anyone's lifestyle and income expectations to be unmet when they realize they didn't pick a financially beneficial degree.

If you've already gotten your degree there's nothing you can do about the amount you borrowed or the degree you got.

The upcoming chapters will cover repayment plans, refinancing, and loan forgiveness to help you find the best combination that will minimize your financial struggle and make your student loans truly repayable.

Chapter 3

●　●　●

Ways to Repay

Repayment plans, they're the starting point of your student loan repayment journey. Most of the time you spend five minutes in the financial aid counselor's office and they look at you and ask "What repayment plan do you want?"

You stare wildly back at them like "I don't know... Which one do you think I should pick?"

They of course offer generalities about what most students choose and you pick your plan so they can move on to their next appointment.

It's not a particularly informative experience. It's really just a box to check before you graduate.

Choosing the right repayment plan can help you repay your loans while keeping the right amount of money back for yourself to suit your lifestyle.

A good payment plan can keep you from worrying that you won't be able to make your monthly payment.

This chapter will help you choose the plan that makes the most sense for you.

No more worrying you're making a stupid financial decision. You will know the ins and outs of each repayment plan and be able to share that information with your younger siblings and your friends who are repaying their loans.

You can finally set up your repayment plan so you can pay your debt back and have a clean slate. You don't have to feel remorse every time you spend money.

I will take you through each of the federal repayment plans and highlight a few key areas: duration of repayment, loan forgiveness options the repayment plan qualifies you for, how the required payments will stack up to your income, pros and cons of the repayment plan, and the target borrower for the plan.

Standard Repayment Plan

<u>What it is:</u> You will make fixed monthly payments for a certain duration

<u>Duration of repayment:</u> 10 years or up to 30 years for Consolidation Loans.

<u>Loan Forgiveness Options:</u> None

Payment compared to income: depends on your total loan amount. Essentially the 10 year plan is the fastest and least expensive (in total payments made) plan because the required monthly payment leads to the loan being repaid in 10 years. This plan also has the highest monthly payments.

<u>Pros:</u> Fastest repayment option with the least amount of interest paid

<u>Cons:</u> If you have a high debt amount your monthly required payments will be high. For example mine were ~$1500/month for $132,000 in student loan debt.

<u>Target borrower:</u> Folks who have a low debt:income ratio are ideal candidates because the required monthly payments won't eat up all the money they need to live off of.

Graduated Repayment Plan

<u>What it is:</u> Payments are initially lower but increase gradually (typically every two years)

<u>Duration of Repayment:</u> 10 years or up to 30 years for Consolidated Loans

<u>Loan Forgiveness Options:</u> None

<u>Payment compared to income:</u> With lower payments first ideally your payments grow in proportion to your income. So when you're making starting pay the payment is lower than when you have experience and get paid for that.

<u>Pros:</u> Lower payments early on

<u>Cons:</u> payments increase as time goes on (independent of your income), you will pay more in total than a standard repayment plan

<u>Target borrower:</u> a borrower who knows their initial income will be low and that it will increase substantially with time

Extended Repayment Plan

<u>What it is:</u> A payment plan that extends the period of time you have to repay an outstanding debt of >$30,000.

<u>Duration of Repayment:</u> Up to 25 years.

<u>Loan Forgiveness Options:</u> None

<u>Payment compared to income:</u> Payments can either be fixed or graduated so you may be able to have lower payments initially when you're making less money and then ramp payments up as you make more money.

<u>Pros:</u> It allows for an extended repayment period for large amounts of debt, your monthly payments will be lower than a 10 year repayment plan.

<u>Cons:</u> You will pay more in total (due to interest) than under the standard 10 year-repayment plan, you will carry your student loan debt for longer.

Target borrower: Borrowers with > $30,000 in student loan debt, folks with high debt:income ratios.

Revised Pay as You Earn Repayment Plan (REPAYE)

<u>What it is:</u> Your monthly payments are 10% of your discretionary income. Payments are recalculated annually based on current income and family size. If your spouse has student loan debt it takes into account the balance of both of your outstanding student loan debt as well as both incomes whether you file joint or separate tax returns.

<u>Duration of Repayment:</u> Up to 20-25 years.

<u>Loan Forgiveness Options:</u> If you have a remaining student loan balance after 20 or 25 years of making payments, that remaining balance will be forgiven. Eligible for Public Service Loan Forgiveness (PSLF).

<u>Payment compared to income:</u> 10% of discretionary income

<u>Pros:</u> Affordable payments, takes into account spouse's income and student loan debt regardless of whether you file a joint tax return.

<u>Cons:</u> May have to carry debt for 20-25 years, may be taxed on the loan balance forgiven, your monthly payment could be more than a 10 year repayment plan if you have a high income.

<u>Target borrower:</u> People with very high debt:income ratio who are unable to afford payments under other plan types and would benefit from forgiveness of the loan balance after 20-25 years of making payments.

Pay as You Earn Repayment Plan (PAYE)

<u>What it is:</u> Your maximum monthly payments will be 10% of your discretionary income. Payments are

recalculated annually based on current income and family size. If your spouse has student loan debt it takes into account the balance of both of your outstanding student loans as well as both incomes only if you file joint tax returns.

Duration of Repayment: Up to 20 years

Loan Forgiveness Options: Any outstanding student loan balance will be forgiven after 20 years of payments. Eligible for Public Service Loan Forgiveness (PSLF)

Payment compared to income: Maximum 10% of discretionary income.

Pros: Affordable payments, forgiveness of remaining balance after 20 years, your monthly payment will never be more than the standard 10 year repayment amount.

Cons: Only takes into account spouse's income and student loan debt if you file a joint tax return, may be taxed on the loan balance forgiven.

Target borrower: You must be a new borrower on or after Oct 1st 2007. You must also demonstrate a high debt:income ratio.

Income-Based Repayment Plan (IBR)

<u>What it is:</u> Monthly payments will be 10 or 15% of discretionary income. You'll pay 10% if you're a new borrower after July 1 2014 and 15% if you're not a new borrower after July 1 2014. Payments are recalculated annually based on current income and family size. If your spouse has student loan debt it takes into account the balance of both of your outstanding student loan debt as well as both incomes only if you file joint tax returns.

<u>Duration of Repayment:</u> 20 or 25 years

<u>Loan Forgiveness Options:</u> remaining balance forgiven after 20 or 25 years and is eligible for PSLF

<u>Payment compared to income:</u> 10 or 15 % of discretionary income, monthly payment will never be more than the standard 10 year repayment amount. You must have high debt:income to qualify.

<u>Pros:</u> Affordable monthly payments, payments never greater than 10 year repayment amount, forgiveness of remaining balance after 20 or 25 years.

<u>Cons:</u> Loan amount forgiven may be taxed, spouse's debt and income will only be considered if you file joint tax return.

<u>Target borrower:</u> Borrowers with a high debt:income ratio.

** A brief interruption here: you might be wondering what the difference is between REPAYE, PAYE, and IBR** At first glance they seem like the same exact payment plan. Here's a table of important differences.

	Spousal Income and Debt		Eligible Borrowers
REPAYE	Taken into account regardless of whether you file a joint tax return	REPAYE	Any borrower with an eligible loan type
PAYE	Only taken into account if you file a joint tax return	PAYE	You must be a new borrower on or after Oct. 1, 2007, and must have received a disbursement of a Direct Loan on or after Oct. 1, 2011.
IBR	Only taken into account if you file a joint tax return		You must have a high debt:income ratio
Maximum Monthly Payment		IBR	You must have a high debt:income ratio
REPAYE	10% of discretionary income		**Duration of Repayment**
PAYE	10% of discretionary income, but no more than the monthly payment under the standard 10 year repayment plan	REPAYE	20-25 years
		PAYE	20 years
IBR	10% of discretionary income, but no more than the monthly payment under the standard 10 year repayment plan	IBR	20 or 25 years

Income-Contingent Repayment Plan (ICR)

<u>What it is:</u> Your monthly payment is the lesser of 20% of discretionary income or your monthly payment on a 12-year repayment plan, adjusted for income.

Payments are recalculated annually based on current income and family size.

<u>Duration of Repayment:</u> up to 25 years

<u>Loan Forgiveness Options</u>: The remaining balance is forgiven after 25 years of repayment, eligible for PSLF.

<u>Payment compared to income:</u> 20 % of discretionary income or the monthly amount of a 12-year fixed re-payment plan, whichever is less.

<u>Pros:</u> affordable payments, compromises speed of re-payment with affordability

<u>Cons:</u> Forgiven balance may be taxed.

<u>Target borrower:</u> Someone who is looking to balance speed of repayment with affordability.

Income-Sensitive Repayment Plan

<u>What it is:</u> Your monthly payment is determined by your income. The formula for calculating your monthly payment can vary from lender to lender.

<u>Duration of Repayment:</u> Up to 15 years

<u>Loan Forgiveness Options:</u> none

<u>Payment compared to income:</u> If your income goes up your payments go up however the formulas for monthly payments differ by lender.

<u>Pros:</u> A compromise of quick repayment and affordability.

<u>Cons:</u> Exact amount you will pay monthly is lender dependent.

<u>Target borrower:</u> Someone who wants affordable payments and has a middle of the road debt:income.

How can I change my payment plan?

Maybe you've read this chapter and realized you want to change payment plans. Your current plan isn't the best one for your financial situation.

Fear not, you can change your repayment plan at any time for no charge.

Changing your payment plan requires contacting your loan servicer. To find out who your loan servicer is, log in to <u>My Federal Student Aid</u>.

I find the most effective means of contact with many loan servicers is on the phone. Fair warning, it will be a pain in the butt and take you more time than you think it should. You will probably spend some time on hold too.

I've found email and other forms of communication don't produce results. It's like nothing ever gets done or changes.

Depending on which payment plan you switch to, you will likely need to provide current income data. You will also likely need to submit other documentation, so if you're somewhere that you can scan or fax a document that's helpful.

Some loan servicers offer you the opportunity to upload pictures and documents to their website so sometimes just having your phone is good enough.

It's hard to know which loan servicers are stuck in the stone age and which have moved into the modern age where no one owns a printer.

Either way it's about an hour's worth of work and totally worth having a repayment plan that suits your financial needs.

Should I consolidate my loans?

Loan consolidation is free and offers borrowers the chance to make payments to only one loan servicer if they currently have loans with multiple servicers.

Loan consolidation is not necessarily the best option for everyone. So how do you know if it's right for you?

You can't consolidate private loans. You are only able to consolidate loans made through the Department of Education (i.e. Direct loans, Perkins loans, and Stafford loans).

Consolidating your loans may give you up to 30 years to repay your balance and make your monthly payments lower. If you choose to repay your loans over a longer time period you will pay more over the term of your loan.

When you consolidate your loans you can lose some of the benefits tied to the original loans. Your interest rate discounts, principle rebates, and some loan cancellation benefits could be lost when you consolidate.

It's important to ask these questions up front so you can be sure that losing these benefits after consolidation doesn't leave you paying more.

A benefit of loan consolidation is that you can consolidate loans with variable interest rates and get a fixed interest rate. This can provide additional security if you are looking at a long repayment term (like 30 years).

Direct Consolidation Loans have a fixed interest rate for the life of the loan. The interest rate is determined based on the weighted averages of the interest rates of the loans being consolidated.

If you have loans at different interest rates you'll want to know the interest rate you will get on your consolidated loan and decide if it will be similar or if it will cost you more.

If you've decided to consolidate your loans go to studentloans.gov and log in. There you can electronically complete the Loan Consolidation application and promissory note. If you want to talk to someone about consolidation you can call the Loan Consolidation Information Call Center at 1-800-557-7392.

When it comes to loan consolidation studentaid.gov does a good job explaining the process and helping you navigate. You can access that information at https://studentaid.ed.gov/sa/repay-loans/consolidation.

Student Loan Debt Case #1

I'm going to run through a real student loan debt case to give you an idea of how the different repayment decisions (repayment plan and loan consolidation) look in real life, with a real person, who has a real career as a nurse.

*Names and identities have been changed to protect borrower's privacy**

Javon Brown is a 27 yo male who graduated with his master's in nursing in 2014. Read through his case below:

<u>What year did you graduate college?</u>
I finished the MSN program in 2014, BSN in 2012, ADN in 2011.

<u>How much student loan debt did you have upon graduation?</u>
My total student loan debt upon graduation was $63,457.

<u>What was your maximum annual loan amount that you borrowed and what year was that?</u>
I took out $20,000 in 2012 at the beginning of my MSN program.

<u>What degree did you graduate with?</u>
Masters of Science in Nursing

<u>What were you getting paid when you first started repaying your loan?</u>
I was salaried so my first year was $52,000 (I only work nine months of the year plus get holiday breaks).

<u>What repayment plan(s) have you used and what is the required monthly payment?</u>
I just do a standard 10 year plan, if I would consolidate then it makes me ineligible to qualify for student loan repayment through HRSA (Health Resources and Services Administration).

<u>What is your general attitude toward student loan repayment? (i.e. repay as quickly as possible, pay the minimum, etc)</u>
My current thought is to pay these frocks off as fast as I can.

<u>What is your current salary?</u>
My salaried spot is $55,321 but I also do nursing work per diem so I should gross about $75,000

<u>When do you expect to have your student loans re-paid or when did you pay them off?</u>
I have a little over $52,000 left so if I get the student loan repayment they will cover 60% over the next two years and then 25% for a third year. If I would receive this I hope to have all student loans done in 3 years with their contribution and mine. If not then I'm praying for 7 years.

<u>What does your monthly budget look like? (income and fixed expenses are most important).</u>
Fixed expenses currently $1,000 home-(includes taxes and insurance in escrow), $220-cell, $425-car, $320-car insurance (every three months), $704-student loans (if I don't pay extra), $32.33-garbage. My variable expenses that I cover are groceries which now runs $400 approximately since we started eating a lot healthier (damn why can't veggies cost as much as Mac and cheese :-) but it depends on what I can find on sale.

I budget out $2,750 for expenses and if I find stuff cheaper I can save that if not that's an approximate of what I spend. I am refinancing our home so that payment will go up slightly by about $50 but then I'll only have to pay on it for 20 years rather than 30 and my interest will go down about 1.125%.

Alright Javon seems to have his head wrapped around his student loan debt.

Let's start our assessment by assessing our baseline situation, which is the debt:income ratio.

Javon's debt:income ratio is calculated by taking his total debt of $63,457 and comparing it to his annual salary, I'll use his assessment of ~$75K gross.

This gives us a debt:income ratio of 0.85:1. This is a very healthy debt to income ratio. So looking back at all of our repayment plan options let's examine the plans that are best-suited to someone with a low debt:income ratio.

We can immediately rule out any of the income-adjusted repayment plans. The majority of the plans (PAYE, IBR) require high debt:income ratio. They also will take longer to pay off than a standard 10-year repayment plan.

Javon's perspective on student loans is that he just wants to knock them out as quickly as possible. That means that although his student loan amount is >$30,000 and he would be eligible for the extended repayment plan, it doesn't meet his personal financial goals.

The remaining payment plan that suits his financial needs and personal goals is the 10 year standard repayment plan.

He mentions that he was not able to consolidate his loans because that would make him ineligible for loan repayment assistance through HRSA. It's important to look into the impact of loan consolidation prior to making that decision.

One of the best ways to learn more about loan consolidation is to read the financial aid website's section on loan consolidation https://studentaid.ed.gov/sa/repay-loans/consolidation and then to give the Loan Consolidation Information Call Center a ring at 1-800-557-7392.

Once you consolidate your loans you can't go back so you want to make sure it's the right decision.

Now that you've seen a real-life example that thinks through how to choose a repayment plan you can start to get an idea for the main things that go into the decision.

Your action step for this chapter is to calculate your debt:income ratio.

If you want to take it a step further and apply this information to take charge or your student loan debt you've got work to do.

Determine which payment plan suits both your financial needs and personal goals. If you decide you should switch repayment plans, contact your loan servicer and do it.

If you're wondering about loan consolidation go to the student aid website and read up on direct consolidation loans then contact their information call center.

That's it, you're informed and making strategic, calculated decisions about the financial impact your student loans will have on you.

It's up to you to enact the changes necessary to line your payment plan up with your #repaymentgoals.

Chapter 4

●　●　●

Reconsider Your Rates

If you've graduated college recently, you know one thing for certain, student loan interest rates are incredibly high, crippling almost. Federal student loan interest rates peaked at around 6.8%. They've come down slightly in recent years.

The problem with student loan interest rates is that borrowers have no credit, no income, and only the promise of building these things. That means whatever the federal student loan interest rate is set at you get. Everyone gets it. I don't know many 18 year olds who have much for a credit history.

However once you graduate there is something big you can do. You can take advantage of the time you spent in college building a credit history. You can take advantage of your shiny new income when you graduate.

How do you take advantage of your new financial strengths?

Refinance your student loans.

By refinancing for a lower interest rate you get to keep more of your money for doing the fun stuff you like. You can stop wasting thousands of dollars on interest and have that money work for you to pay off your debt faster.

This chapter will ensure you avoid refinancing pitfalls so you don't get caught in a scam or find yourself without the important safety nets provided by federal loans.

Jeni what if my information isn't safe? I don't want to give someone on the internet my social security number and information!

The companies specifically mentioned in this chapter are legitimate, reputable companies. Think about it like this. Do you own a credit card? You probably applied for it online and gave them access to the same information.

If you're still worried about security, email the company's customer service and ask what they do to protect your information. The bonus about emailing the company to ask about security is you will be able to test the quality of their customer service before you refinance with them.

Jeni this seems too good to be true, how can these companies afford to slash my interest rates? What's in it for the refinancing company?

Great question. The refinancing company still gets your interest, potentially thousands to tens of thousands over the life of the loan. Don't forget that student loan debt is the second largest piece of the consumer debt pie at $1.3 trillion. With that kind of money on the table it makes a lot of sense for companies to get into the business of buying them up.

Think about this: if you had the opportunity to buy an investment that earned a 3.4% rate of return annually would you? I know that I certainly would… well, if I didn't have a shit load of student loan debt I mean.

If you're interested in refinancing your student loans but you want to be sure you don't get scammed or miss something important, I get it. Working with a private company that's not the government feels a little sketchy. It's much more obvious that these companies are in it for the profits. So how do you avoid potential pitfalls?

Important Considerations When Choosing a Refinancing Company

Not all refinancing companies are created equally. Some companies offer borrower benefits that are similar to federal student loans while others offer very little. So what should you look for?

Check for loan origination fees. Loan origination fees are what the lender charges you to process your loan, these can cost hundreds to thousands of dollars. There are several refinancing companies that don't charge loan origination fees. Refinance through a company that doesn't charge you to acquire your loan.

Check for application fees. Does it cost you money to apply to refinance your loan? If so look elsewhere, several refinancing companies have free applications so don't waste money here.

Check to see if the lender has early repayment fees. When you refinance many of the lenders will offer you the option of selecting your own monthly payment and repayment term. You will want to find out if they penalize early repayment. If they do charge a fee for early repayment you should find a different company to refinance through.

What happens if you decide you want to go back to school? Some lenders offer deferment for up to three years. Check with the company you're considering to see if they offer any sort of deferment for continued higher education.

If you're definitely planning to return to school you need to strongly consider if refinancing is a good option for you.

You also want to know the benefits that refinancing company offers borrowers in case of financial hardship such as job loss. Does the company offer unemployment protection? Some companies will allow you to enter a period of forbearance ranging anywhere from two to twelve months.

If you die what happens to your newly refinanced loan? If you have federal student loans and die or sustain an injury that leaves you permanently disabled and unable to work to repay your student loans they will be forgiven. That means your loved one won't be responsible for tens of thousands or perhaps hundreds of thousands of dollars od debt.

When you refinance this benefit is often lost. If your loan servicer doesn't offer forgiveness upon death you should be sure to plan and have an appropriate amount of life insurance. You can consider a term policy for the duration of your student loan repayment.

How do you find all this information? Most refinancing companies have good FAQs that contain a lot of this information. They may also have a benefits section.

I still find emailing the customer service department very helpful. I did this to double check some of the most important considerations (like early repayment fees).

Emailing the customer service department gives you a chance to assess their customer service. After everything is considered and you've narrowed it down to companies that meet your criteria and give you similar interest rates, customer service can serve as a deciding factor.

Choosing the Best Interest Rate for You

To find the best interest rate you're going to want to shop around and compare a little bit. Choose from the companies that meet your criteria above. You will want to complete enough of the application to get an estimate of your interest rates.

The information that refinancing companies use to give you better interest rates are your credit score, assets on hand (i.e. 401K, cash), total debt load (mortgage, car payments, etc.), and your income.

Student loan refinancing lenders are typically able to cherry pick their candidates. It has to do with the fact that student loan debt is a $1.3 trillion dollar business in America. That means they can skim the cream off the top by selecting the least risky candidates and still have a very large pool to choose from.

Educations that produce high incomes also tend to cost a lot. So these particular graduates have a good amount of student loan debt.

It's a winning combination for lenders. High amounts of debt mean high amounts of interest (even at reduced rates) which means more money for them. They also select borrowers who are most well-equipped to repay their loans so they end up being fairly low-risk.

So what makes you a good candidate for refinancing? Someone who will get much lower interest rates?

You need to have excellent credit. Lenders are also looking for a good income profile. Some lenders may limit to institution (i.e. college you attended).

If you've applied to refinance and have a few interest rates to compare between different lenders you might have a question… how do you know if you should choose a fixed vs. variable interest rate?

The variable interest rates are often lower than the fixed interest rate by 1-1.5%. It's pretty tempting to go after the lowest interest rate, but what are the risks? How do you know if you should go for that lower interest rate?

To help you decide I'm going to give you a brief lesson in fixed vs. variable interest rates.

A fixed interest rate is one that does not change throughout the life of the loan. So no matter what happens with the economy or financial markets your interest rate remains fixed.

A variable interest rate is one that changes based on current financial markets. If you're considering a variable interest rate you'll want to know which financial index your lender bases their variable interest rate on. Some lenders base their interest rates off the LIBOR index.

Knowing the index your variable rate is based on can give you information about how stable your interest rate might be.

After you've looked at the objective information available regarding your financial markets the decision is largely based on personal preference.

Some things you should consider include the term of your repayment. Do you plan to make payments for a long time or are you trying to repay your loan as quickly as possible? The shorter the amount of time you plan to repay the less likely you are to encounter a sky-rocketing interest rate. In other words the variable interest rate is less "risky".

Student Loan Debt Case #2

Names and identities have been changed to protect the borrower's privacy Read through the following case for a closer examination of difference between fixed and variable interest rates.

Seon Li is a 29 yo female pharmacist. Her case is presented below.

What year did you graduate college?
I graduated with my undergraduate degree in 2009 and Pharm.D in 2013.

How much student loan debt did you have upon graduation?
I finished my bachelor's with about $10,000 in debt. With the addition of pharmacy school I graduated with a total debt of $165,000.

What was your maximum student loan debt load and what year was that?
$175,000 in 2013.

What degree did you graduate with?
Pharm.D.

<u>What were you getting paid when you first started repaying your loan?</u>
I earned $107,000 after I completed a pharmacy residency, during my year of residency I earned ~$45,000.

<u>What repayment plan(s) have you used and what is the required monthly payment?</u>
I am using IBR and the payments are approximately $1,100 a month.

<u>What is your general attitude toward student loan repayment? (i.e. repay as quickly as possible, pay the minimum, etc)</u>
I have mixed feelings. Yes I would like to pay my student loans back as soon as possible. The problem is I think taking opportunities when you are young is much better than waiting until we are older. Over the past three years since graduation I have been able to travel a lot and those are experiences I will never forget. In hindsight there were many items I didn't need to spend money on. Like the cup of coffee at Starbucks, those add up.

<u>What is your current salary?</u>
$120,000

<u>When do you expect to have your student loans repaid or when did you pay them off?</u>
No idea. Hopefully using the PSLF for 10 years and have the loans forgiven after 10 years. However, it is scary to count on that because you never know if the program will still be there or if they will max the amount that can be forgiven.

<u>What does your monthly budget look like? (income and fixed expenses are most important).</u>
I don't actually keep a budget. Every time I start one I lose motivation after a week or two. I hope to eventually keep a budget.

Alright Seon seems to have a little bit different a viewpoint on student loan debt than our previous case Javon. Seon specifically mentions travel and experiences as very important to her.

Let's run her student loan debt through four interest rate scenarios. Each scenario will be the $175,000 repaid over 15 years, however, the interest rate will either be her original federal loan rate of 6.7%, a fixed interest rate, a variable interest rate that remains low, or a variable interest rate that eventually reaches the interest rate cap.

Federal Student Loan Fixed Interest Rate

Seon's interest rate in repayment is not based on her credit score. Interest rates upon graduation in 2013 were 6.8% however Seon was able to get her rate discounted to 6.7% by signing up for automatic payments. This makes her monthly payment $1,543.74 for 15 years. She will pay $102,874.58 in interest during the 15 years she spends in repayment.

Fixed interest rate loan

Seon makes a good income and has good credit. When she goes to refinance her student loans she is approved for a fixed interest rate of 4.8%. This makes her monthly payment $1,365.73 for 15 years. She will pay $70,830.15 of interest during her 15 years she spends in repayment.

Variable interest rate loan that remains steadily low

Because of Seon's good income and credit she is able to qualify for a 3.36% interest rate if she chooses to refinance. We're going to run through a best case scenario that assumes the interest rate doesn't fluctuate above her previous rate. This makes her monthly payment $1,239.05 for 15 years. She will pay $48,208 in interest during the 15 years she spends in repayment.

<u>Variable interest rate loan that reaches the lender's pre-determined cap of 10%</u>

Let's say the odds are not forever in Seon's favor and interest rates skyrocket over the course of her repayment terms. She will start out with an interest rate of 3.36% and end with an interest rate of 10%. Her monthly payment will start out at $1,239.05 however it will increase with each interest rate increase. I have assumed that the interest rate increases annually at a rate of 0.44. Seon will pay $81,397 in interest during the 15 years she spends in repayment.

All the options Seon has available look like this:

	Total Interest Paid
Federal Loans at 6.7%	$102,874
Fixed Rate Loan at 4.8%	$70,830
Variable Rate Loan at 3.36%	$48,208
Variable Rate Loan starting at 3.36% and increasing to 10%	$81,397

For Seon the worst financial option is to continue repaying her loans under the federal interest rate of 6.7%. The decision between a fixed interest rate and a variable interest rate is a little bit trickier.

Because the fixed interest rate is relatively close to the variable interest rate it is possible that if her variable interest rates reach capped amounts Seon could pay more interest than if she refinanced with a fixed rate loan.

Variable interest rates have not been that high since 1989. The likelihood of interest rates sky-rocketing to those levels is dubious. It is something to consider along with the fact that as those interest rates increased so would the monthly payment.

Another thing to consider is that interest rates would have to steadily rise to the point of 10% interest. If they remain low for even a few years with relatively small increase then Seon will spend less money on interest up front and will have paid down more principle so a later increase in interest has less of an impact on Seon's total interest paid.

A lot of the decision to choose a variable vs. fixed rate loan has to do with your personal level of comfort with financial risk.

For some of you the idea that your interest rate might increase could motivate you to put extra money toward your student loans and pay them off more quickly.

For others the thought that your interest rate might increase could keep you awake at night. If you fall in this camp you might be much happier paying a little extra interest and keeping your sanity.

The shorter your loan term the more appealing a variable interest rate is. It means you have yourself set up to repay your debt quickly and will quickly decrease the amount of principal on your loan. When interest rates do increase they will have a smaller impact because you have less loan left and have already saved a lot of money up front with the lower interest rate.

Either way, fixed or variable interest rate, you will save money compared to your federal student loan rate so refinancing is a must. Remember that worst case scenario variable interest rate? It still saved you $21,477 compared to the federal rate. You could buy a new economy car for that kind of money.

So whether you choose a fixed or variable interest rate loan you will save more money than if you were paralyzed by doubt and chose to stick with your federal loan interest rate.

Why doesn't everyone refinance?

Some candidates look better to lenders than others. Seon was an ideal candidate because she had great credit and a high income. These make her a "low-risk" investment from a lender's viewpoint. People like Seon with good credit scores and high incomes will get good interest rates.

Remember, Seon didn't actually refinance her loans. She's doing an income-based repayment plan and is paying 6.7% interest still.

Why is that?

Seon qualifies for Public Service Loan Forgiveness (PSLF) which we'll discuss in detail in the next chapter.

Anyone who qualifies for a loan forgiveness program should very carefully assess the numbers for their various options, repayment plans, loan forgiveness, and refinancing and choose the option that saves them the most money.

If you're going to take advantage of a loan forgiveness program, DO NOT REFINANCE. Refinancing will make you ineligible for loan forgiveness options. Loan forgiveness programs only forgive federal student loans. When you refinance, your federal loans are sold and you now have private loans.

You also need to be cautious about consolidating your loans. Not all loan forgiveness programs will forgive Direct Consolidation Loans. If you consolidate your loans you may no longer qualify for certain loan forgiveness programs.

For many people, loan refinancing is a great option that can save you a lot of money in interest. Once you've decided refinancing is right for you, there are a few big considerations.

Which lender has the best options for me?

The best lender has a combination of the lowest interest rate and the best borrower benefits (like deferment, zero loan origination fees, and no early repayment fees).

A few reputable lenders to consider are Earnest, SoFi, and any of the lenders vetted through credible.com. I personally chose Earnest because they have excellent borrower benefits, great customer service, and offered me the lowest interest rate.

When you do your homework, if you decide Earnest is the best company for you, use this link https://www.earnest.com/invite/jennifer2390 and we'll both get $200.

Once you've chosen a lender it's time to decide between a fixed and variable interest rate loan. This decision is based on the term of your repayment and your personal tolerance for risk.

Refinancing is a smart way to make your monthly payments work more efficiently to pay down your student loan debt. It comes with no additional personal sacrifice and enables you to pay less in interest. It keeps more of your money in your pocket.

If refinancing is something you're interested in here's your homework. Go to credible.com, Sofi.com, and ear to check out the borrower benefits of multiple lenders. If you run into trouble contact their customer service department. Choose your top 3-5 lenders and submit applications for interest rate estimates. Then compare the offered interest rates to your benefits and choose a refinancing company.

Once you've refinanced you can bask in the glory of watching your student loan debt shrink rapidly!

Please Forgive Them.

Chapter 5

Please Forgive Them

Your student loan debt amount is ridiculously high. Your debt:income ratio is practically crushing you and you feel like you'll never be able to get out from under the burden of student loan debt.

What are you going to do?

You may not have to repay your student loan debt amount in its entirety. Some of it may be forgiven, and you might save thousands.

Forgiveness programs can minimize the impact student loan debt has on your life. You might not have to choose between putting yourself in financial stress to make your payments and paying on your loans forever.

I'm going to be up front about the loan forgiveness options that are currently available. The vast majority of these programs are for folks in healthcare, teaching, or public service of some sort. So if you're not in one of these fields you don't have a lot of loan forgiveness options.

There are some forgiveness options, based on duration of repayment, that are available to all borrowers with federal loans. Even if your career isn't one of public service, keep reading to learn the details of the federal forgiveness options.

Each loan forgiveness option will talk about which loans qualify, which borrowers qualify, any stipulations on maximum amount forgiven, and any taxes on the forgiven loan amount.

How do I know if I have federal or private loans?

Good question, before we walk about different forgiveness options you'll need to know which type of student loans you have.

The best place to find your federal student loan amount is to log onto the National Student Loan

Data System (NSLDS). This database will only list federal student loans.

Private loans are made by a variety of lenders and banks, not the government. Federal loans are the only loans that qualify for forgiveness.

Public Service Loan Forgiveness (PSLF)

<u>What it does:</u> PSLF forgives the remaining balance on your Direct Loans after you have made 120 qualifying monthly payments under a qualifying repayment plan while working full-time for a qualifying employer.[12]

<u>Why the program exists:</u> PSLF, created in 2007, was started to relieve the pressure of high student loan debt for borrowers working in public service where pay is often lower than private sector work.

<u>Borrower Eligibility:</u> The specific job you do doesn't determine your eligibility. Eligibility is determined by your employer. If you work for a government organization (federal, state, local, or tribal) your employer qualifies. If you work for a not-for-profit company

---

12 https://studentaid.ed.gov/sa/repay-loans/forgiveness-cancellation/public-service

that's tax exempt under 501(c)(3) of the IRS code you qualify. Other types of non-profits that provide certain qualifying public services are also eligible. Check out this link https://studentaid.ed.gov/sa/glossary#Qualifying_Public_Services for a list of qualifying employers.

Qualifying loans: Federal Direct Loans, Direct Consolidation Loans (your 120 payments will start from the time of consolidation).

Maximum Forgiveness Amount: No maximum forgiveness amount.

Tax Information: Forgiven loan amount is not taxed.

Jeni, I'm doing the math and no one has actually gotten loans forgiven through PSLF yet, could PSLF disappear?

The first borrowers who qualify for PSLF will be eligible for forgiveness in October of 2017. It's difficult to know if PSLF will undergo change as loan balances are forgiven for eligible borrowers.

Here's an unhelpful quote...

"The Department [of education] cannot make any guarantees regarding the future availability of

PSLF. The PSLF Program was created by Congress, and, while not likely, Congress could change or end the PSLF Program."

Yep it's really that straightforward. Congress could vote and repeal PSLF. Some folks have suggested that there could be a class action lawsuit by borrowers against the government but I'm not sure about that. Technically no one in this program is eligible for anything until 120 payments have been made. So there's nothing being promised and then not delivered...

In 2015 President Obama proposed capping the amount of loan forgiveness at $57,000. The Republican Party has proposed stopping the program all together. However the cap and cancelling the program have been quiet for a little while so I think you're safe from both... for now.

So how do you decide if PSLF is right for you?

Financially, deciding if PSLF is right for you is relatively straight forward but requires making a few assumptions.

Calculate the amount you're going to pay over 10 years like this: Monthly payment (in your income-driven repayment plan of choice) X 120 = the total amount you will pay over 10 years.

Huge assumption number one is that you will make the same income and therefore payment. This is unlikely because you will probably get raises over 10 years and your payments will slowly increase.

The second assumption is that you will be continuously working full-time for an eligible employer. If you take breaks between jobs or work a stretch for an ineligible employer you could seriously reduce the amount of loans forgiven because payments made during that time won't count toward your 120.

If the amount you calculate is significantly less than the amount you owe, for example if you owe $150K and you calculate you'll repay $110K on an income-based plan, then it might make financial sense for you to do it.

The personal considerations can be more challenging. Can you get out of debt faster on your own? If your income enables you to pay enough each month to shorten your repayment period by years then I propose that's the route you take.

Nothing in this payment plan is a guarantee and holding onto debt comes at its own cost. It leads to the cliched stuff like delaying marriage, first home, and kids. But it also leads to more subtle entrapment.

You may feel trapped in a certain type of employment or at a specific job or employer. Even if your job isn't meeting your needs you may stay for the sake of loan forgiveness.

If PSLF gets revoked you essentially handed yourself a bunch of interest. All it takes is a vote by Congress who doesn't often vote for positive changes for the cost of education (if you don't believe me see rising costs of tuition, outrageous federal interest rates, and the student debt doomsday clock).

You could hope that existing participants would be grandfathered in. However, 10 years is a long time to make payments. If this were to be revoked you would end up paying a lot more than if you went after your debt early.

If you have private loans you need to carefully examine what loan amount will actually be paid off. The only loans that qualify are Direct Loans. Not Perkins, FFEL, or health professionals loans. IF you want those loans to qualify consolidate them into a Direct Consolidation Loan early. You will then have to make 120 payments on that consolidation loan to be eligible for forgiveness and any previous payments made wouldn't count.

Teacher Loan Forgiveness

<u>What it does:</u> If you teach full-time for five complete and consecutive academic years in certain elementary and secondary schools and educational service agencies that serve low-income families, and meet other qualifications, you may be eligible for forgiveness of up to a combined total of $17,500 on your Direct Subsidized and Unsubsidized Loans and your Subsidized and Unsubsidized Federal Stafford Loans.[13]

<u>Why the program exists:</u> Teacher loan forgiveness is designed to encourage individuals to enter and continue in the teaching profession.

<u>Borrower Eligibility:</u> You must have been employed as a full-time teacher for five complete and consecutive academic years, and at least one of those years

---

13 https://studentaid.ed.gov/sa/repay-loans/forgiveness-cancellation/teacher

must have been after the 1997–98 academic year, in an elementary or secondary school that serves low-income students. See directory[14]

Qualifying loans: Direct Subsidized and Unsubsidized Loans and your Subsidized and Unsubsidized Federal Stafford Loans.

Maximum Forgiveness Amount: $17,500

Tax Information: Unclear if the amount forgiven is taxed as income.

Teacher Cancellation for Federal Perkins Loans

What it does: Cancels up to 100% of remaining loan balance on Federal Perkins Loans for full-time teaching at a low-income school, or for teaching in certain subject area.

Why the program exists: To encourage individuals to enter and continue in the teaching profession.

Borrower Eligibility: You are eligible after one year of full-time teaching in a low-income school, or if you teach special education, or if you teach a designated shortage subject.[15]

---

14 https://www.tcli.ed.gov/CBSWebApp/tcli/TCLIPubSchoolSearch.jsp
15 http://www2.ed.gov/about/offices/list/ope/pol/tsa.pdf

<u>Qualifying loans:</u> Federal Perkins Loans

<u>Maximum Forgiveness Amount:</u> Up to 100% of the loans in increments over five years; 15% for years one and two of service, 20% for years three and four, and 30% for year five.

<u>Tax Information:</u> Loan amount is cancelled so it's not taxed.

IBR, PAYE, REPAYE, ICR Loan Forgiveness

<u>What it does:</u> Forgives the remaining loan balance after 20 years or 25 years of consistent payments depending on the specific repayment plan and when you borrowed.[16]

<u>Why the program exists:</u> To forgive the remaining student loan balance after many years of consistent repayment.

<u>Borrower Eligibility:</u> IBR and PAYE require the payment you would be required to make under the IBR plan (based on your income and family size) must be less than what you would pay under the Standard Repayment Plan with a 10-year repayment period.

---

16 https://studentaid.ed.gov/sa/sites/default/files/income-driven-repayment.pdf

REPAYE and ICR loan forgiveness is available to any borrower with eligible loans.

Qualifying loans: Vary by plan. Direct loans made to students (subsidized, unsubsidized, consolidation, and PLUS) are eligible under all plans. In general Stafford loans are eligible only under IBR or if they're consolidated to a direct loan under the other repayment plans.

Maximum Forgiveness Amount: None

Tax Information: Taxed as income

Nurse Faculty Loan Program (NFLP)

What it does: Funds are distributed to public or private nonprofit accredited schools of nursing offering educator coursework as part of an advanced education nursing degree program(s) that prepares students to serve as nurse faculty.

Why the program exists: increase the number of qualified nursing faculty by providing funding to accredited schools of nursing.

Borrower Eligibility: It is up to individual colleges to create and manage a loan forgiveness program with a revolving loan fund component.

NURSE Corp Loan Forgiveness

<u>What it does:</u> sets registered nurses (including advanced practice registered nurses and nursing faculty) on a rewarding career path while paying off 60 percent of their unpaid nursing student loans in just 2 years – plus an additional 25 percent of the original balance for an optional third year.[17]

<u>Why the program exists:</u> to assist in the recruitment and retention of professional Registered Nurses (RNs), including advanced practice RNs, who are dedicated to working in eligible health care facilities with a critical shortage of nurses or eligible schools of nursing.

<u>Borrower Eligibility:</u> You must be a licensed registered nurse (nurse practitioners and other advanced practice nurses are encouraged to apply) or nurse faculty, have completed your training (diploma, associate, baccalaureate or graduate), and be employed full time (at least 32 hours per week) at an eligible critical shortage facility.

<u>Qualifying loans:</u> Federal Loans made directly to the student. Perkins loans are ineligible unless borrower can demonstrate that they are not subject to cancellation.

---

17 http://www.hrsa.gov/loanscholarships/repayment/nursing/

<u>Maximum Forgiveness Amount:</u> No cap, 30% of total qualifying loan amount the first two years, plus an additional 25% for an optional third year of service.

<u>Tax Information:</u> Federal income tax and Federal Insurance Contributions Act (FICA) tax (Social Security and Medicare) are withheld from a participant's award. These taxes are paid directly to the IRS on the participant's behalf.

Other Profession and State-specific Loan Forgiveness Programs

I'm aware of loan forgiveness options for the following professions: teachers, doctors, and lawyers, based on state. The best way to find these forgiveness options is to google your profession, loan forgiveness, and state. So for example I would google "pharmacist loan forgiveness in Wisconsin".

A Word About Taxes on Forgiven Loan Amounts

For the income-based loan forgiveness and a few of the other loan forgiveness options the loan amount forgiven is taxable. That means that you have to report it as income.

Depending on your tax bracket you could owe over $10,000 in taxes for loan forgiveness of $40,000. If you're going to utilize a loan forgiveness program that taxes forgiven amounts be sure to save and prepare for that tax bill.

A CPA or tax accountant can help you estimate more closely how much you may owe in taxes.

Student Loan Debt Case #3

Names and identities have been changed to protect the borrower's privacy Read through the following case for a closer examination of difference between fixed and variable interest rates.

Tarik Johnson is a 24 yo male who serves as the program coordinator for student health services at a public university. His case is presented below.

<u>What year did you graduate college?</u>
2014 undergrad 2016 masters in public health.

<u>How much student loan debt did you have upon graduation?</u>
I graduated with about $80,000 in student loan debt

What was your maximum student loan debt load and what year was that?
$85,000 in 2016

What degree did you graduate with?
Master's in public health MPH

What were you getting paid when you first started repaying your loan?
My starting salary is $42,000 although I haven't started repaying my loan just yet, one more month of deferment!

What repayment plan(s) have you used and what is the required monthly payment?
I'm currently deferring my loan repayment for 6 months

What is your general attitude toward student loan repayment? (i.e. repay as quickly as possible, pay the minimum, etc)
I know I have a ton of student loan debt. I'm nervous about how I'm going to pay it all back. For right now I'm deferring, then I'll do an income-based repayment plan.

<u>What is your current salary?</u>
$42,000

<u>When do you expect to have your student loans repaid or when did you pay them off?</u>
I have no idea.

<u>What does your monthly budget look like? (income and fixed expenses are most important).</u>
I don't keep a formal budget. In general I try to save money on unnecessary expenses like clothes, going out, etc. but I enjoy having fun and hanging out with my friends.

Tarik has a large burden of student loan debt compared to income. His debt:income ratio is nearly 2:1. That makes him an ideal candidate for an income-based repayment plan and any loan forgiveness option available to him.

The option we're going to walk through is PSLF. Because Tarik works for a public university which is seen as a government agency, his employer qualifies him for PSLF. Remember, it doesn't matter what type of work you do for that organization, just that you work for an eligible employer.

In order to qualify Tarik needs to pick the best repayment plan. Likely the best option for repayment is the PAYE plan. Tarik is qualified because he was a new borrower after Oct 1st, 2007 and has a high amount of debt relative to his income.

The PAYE plan is a good choice because Tarik will pay 10% of his discretionary income and never pay more than the standard 10 year repayment plan. The estimated monthly payments at Tarik's current salary are $201.50 per month.

Tarik's monthly payment will be adjusted annually based on his income and family size. For ease of estimation we will assume a flat income over the 120 payment required to qualify for PSLF.

Over the 120 payments Tarik makes he will pay $24,180 of his debt. As PSLF exists today the remainder of his student loan will be forgiven tax free.

There are a few things that could change the value of PSLF for Tarik. If he doesn't work for a qualifying employer consistently over 10 years he will pay more money. You don't have to work for a qualifying employer consecutively to qualify for PSLF. But you do have to make 120 qualifying payments. So if you work for a non-qualifying employer for a year (12 payments) you will have to continue making your student loan payments during that time but they won't count toward your PSLF eligibility.

That means, instead of only making 120 payments and then having the balance forgiven, you will make 132 payments.

As of right now PSLF has no cap on the total loan amount that can be forgiven. However, this benefit has not yet been paid out to borrowers. The first borrowers will be eligible in October 2017. It's hard to know how much this loan forgiveness will cost the government.

If a lot of people have high amounts of debt forgiven I anticipate Congress will move to limit the total loan amount forgiven. I also anticipate that if a large amount of loan money is forgiven, Congress will move to tax the forgiven amount.

It's difficult to know if these changes will be grandfathered in or if they will take effect immediately. Technically no borrower is eligible for this type of forgiveness until 120 payments have been made, which takes 10 years. So the government may not be obligated to grandfather anyone in.

All speculation aside, as PSLF currently stands it is the best financial option for Tarik and he should pursue this option for student loan repayment.

The worst case scenario for him is that he ends up having to pay on his student loans for 20 years and has the remaining balance forgiven. If that was the case he would pay $48,360 of the $80,000 he borrowed.

He would still save >$30,000 in student loan debt and interest.

Student loan forgiveness is an especially attractive option for folks with high amounts of debt relative to their income.

If you're considering a student loan debt forgiveness program there are a few things for you to keep in mind.

1. In general, only federal loans are eligible for loan forgiveness.
2. Refinancing your loans makes them private loans and ineligible for forgiveness.
3. Pay attention to your payment plan. Be sure to choose a plan that is eligible for your forgiveness plan of choice and that minimizes the amount you pay out of pocket.

There is an element of social responsibility that I tie in with student loan forgiveness. And it's that if you make good money and can afford to pay your loans off in 10 years without loan forgiveness it's your responsibility to do so.

I know that it sucks, and it comes at a financial sacrifice. I know that you feel like you shouldn't have had to pay that much for college in the first place. I'm not defending the system.

What I'm defending is loan forgiveness for people like Tarik who really need loan forgiveness. If people like me, who make good money and have a reasonable debt:income ratio get tens of thousands of dollars of loans forgiven, just so we essentially don't have to pay interest on our loans, it means there is less money to help those who really need repayment.

I'm not judging you if you make good money and take the loan forgiveness option that you're eligible for. It's there for the taking and likely makes a lot of financial sense.

I'm challenging you to understand the target borrowers for loan forgiveness and think of the impact your loan forgiveness has on the benefit these future borrowers will get. They might have restricted benefits, caps on loan forgiveness amounts, taxed loan forgiveness, or the forgiveness option may disappear altogether.

Chapter 6

The Democracy of Debt

The millennial generation (born 1980-2004) carries the highest generational burden of student loan debt. Interestingly the millennial generation also makes up approximately 31% of the electorate vote.[18]

The financial burden of student loan debt exceeds $1.3 trillion and represents one of the largest financial concerns for this massive voting generation.

With statistics like that you would think student loan debt and the cost of higher education would be at the forefront of every political debate.

18 http://www.pewresearch.org/fact-tank/2016/05/16/millennials-match-baby-boomers-as-largest-generation-in-u-s-electorate-but-will-they-vote/

Other than Senator Bernie Sanders' presidential nominee campaign, higher education has been merely an afterthought, if it's addressed at all. In general there is little legislation designed to help curb the rising costs of college education and ballooning burden of student loan debt.

This chapter will explain the backstory of our government's involvement in funding higher education.

By arming you with historical information you can understand policy trends, perhaps gain insight into political party values, and figure out how to get your student loan debt agenda to be part of the federal agenda.

It's hard to be involved in key discussions and votes on the national scale without knowing what current legislation looks like. Your voice needs to be heard so policy can be made to accommodate the student loan debt burden of the largest living generation.

Policies that make repayment less of a struggle and allow you to keep more of your own money can and should be created for you and our generation.

I know what you're thinking... *Jeni in this political mess my one voice doesn't make a difference or matter to Congress. All politicians care about are big organizations with big money.*

Not true!

We are the largest living generation with over 83 million of us, and we represent 31% of the electorate vote. In a democracy like the U.S. there is massive power in numbers. We just need to organize and unite under a common cause. Be sure to check out *Chapter 10 Make it Viral* for more information and action steps you can take to get the word out about making student loan debt repayable.

Let's start at the beginning, the origination of student loans. In 1958 the National Defense Education Act provided the first direct loans; these loans were capitalized with U.S. Treasury funds.

In 1965 a shift to providing guaranteed loans was made to appease the budget rules of the time. Making direct loans appeared as a loss for that year on the budget while guaranteeing a loan didn't show any upfront budget costs at all.

In 1965 the government started guaranteeing loans made by banks and non-profit lenders. This was the beginning of the Federal Family Education Loan (FFEL) program. This process of guaranteeing private loans without addressing their cost on the budget continued for the next 25 years.

In 1990 President George H.W. Bush signed the Federal Credit Reform Act which was part of a larger bill (The Omnibus Reconciliation Act of 1990). This act required all government agencies to account for the long-term costs of any loans, whether guaranteed loans or loans made directly by a government agency.

As a consequence of the transparency in loan budgeting, the Bush administration analyzed the costs of the loan guarantee program compared to the cost of the government lending money to students directly. The analysis demonstrated that it would be simpler and less costly to directly loan money to students rather than guarantee private loans. In 1992 Congress created a direct lending pilot program.

In 1993, President Clinton proposed replacing guaranteed loans with direct loans. The Omnibus Reconciliation Act of 1993 started phasing in direct loans and phasing out guaranteed loans. The goal was to get 60% of colleges to switch from the guaranteed program to the direct lending program. The act gave the Secretary of Education the power to require colleges to switch to direct lending programs until at least 60% of loans nationwide were direct.

However in 1994 bi-partisan views started to create dissent. A Republican-led congress targeted direct lending for elimination. However, colleges liked the simplicity of the direct lending program. Direct lending eliminated the thousands of middlemen involved in the guaranteed loan program.

Congress did not ultimately eliminate the direct lending program. Instead they passed a law prohibiting the Department of Education from encouraging or requiring colleges to switch to the direct lending program. The goal of this was to maximize the college's choice.

Unfortunately, the number of colleges participating in the direct loan program started to decline. In 2003 a team of investigative reporters at US News & World Report investigated why some colleges were switching back to the guaranteed loan program.

The major finding of this report was that the student loan industry "used money and favors, along with their friends in Congress and the Department of Education to get what they wanted."[19]

In 2005 the Bankruptcy Reform Bill made both private and federal student loans ineligible for discharge in bankruptcy.

In 2007, the attorney general of New York State, Andrew Cuomo, uncovered numerous cases of conflicts of interest between college financial aid officials and student loan lenders.[20] One Senate committee report concluded that "some FFEL lenders provided compensation to schools with the expectation, and in some cases an explicit agreement, that the school will give the lenders preferential treatment, including placement on the school's preferred lender list."[21]

It's unsurprising that an industry with a lot of money exerted influence and questionable ethics to

---

19 Megan Barnett, Julian E. Barnes, and Danielle Knight, "Big Money On Campus: In the Multibillion-dollar World of Student Loans, Big Lenders Are Finding New Ways to Drain Uncle Sam's Coffers," U.S. News & World Report, Oct. 19, 2003

20 Diana J. Schemo, "Cuomo Plans to Broaden Student-Lending Inquiry," New York Times, June 7, 2007

21 U. S. Senate Health, Education, Labor and Pensions Committee, Report on Marketing Practices in the Federal Family Education Loan Program, June 14, 2007http://files.eric.ed.gov/fulltext/ED497127.pdf

continue to benefit their bottom line rather than benefiting the masses.

By 2007 the volume of new loans in the Direct Loan program was the lowest since the program's inception in the 1990's.

However in 2008 the financial market righted wrongs when the credit market crashed. The crash limited the ability of private lenders to make guaranteed loans and many dropped out of the industry.

Schools which had previously participated in the guaranteed loan program switched to the Direct Loan program.

In 2008 the Ensuring Continued Access to Student Loans Act (ECASLA) was passed to temporarily allow the Department of Education to buy up guaranteed loans made by private lenders.

In 2010 Congress passed the Healthcare and Education Reconciliation Act of 2010 which eliminated the FFEL program (the one that guaranteed private loans). As of July 1st 2010 all federal student loans have been made under the Direct Loan program.

Congress estimates $68.7 billion in savings by 2020 which they used to increase funding for the Pell Grant program.

In July 2015 a staff report was published by the Federal Reserve Bank of New York[22] which concluded that institutions exposed to increases in student loan program maximums tend to respond with disproportionate raises in tuition prices.

The Business of Funding

Public colleges and universities educate 68% of the nation's post-secondary students. Revenue from federal and state sources made up 37% of total revenue at public colleges and universities in 2013.

Public post-secondary learning is funded both by the federal government as well as state governments. Historically (from 1987-2012), states contributed about 65% more funding than federal government. In the wake of the Great Recession, state spending on higher education has been cut sharply while federal money (primarily in the form of Pell Grants) has steadily increased.

---

22 Lucca et al "Credit Supply and the Rise in College Tuition: Evidence from the Expansion in Federal Student Aid Programs" Staff Report No. 733 July 2015Revised March 2016 https://www.newyorkfed.org/medialibrary/media/research/staff_reports/sr733.pdf

In 2013, federal spending on major higher education programs totaled $75.6 billion and state spending amounted to $72.7 billion.[23]

Despite nearly identical spending, state and federal money is used in very different ways to fund higher education.

Approximately 73% of state funding is used for general-purpose appropriations while the remaining 27% is split between state financial aid grants and state-funded research.

In contrast approximately 5% of federal money is used for general appropriations, 41% is used for Pell Grants, 33% of funding is used for federal research grants, 16% is used for veteran's education benefits, and the remaining 5% is split between financial aid grants and other grants.

Spending on higher education makes up about 2% of the federal budget but represents the third highest spending category for states, behind elementary and secondary education and Medicaid.

Federal funding for higher education is widely variable among states. The national average for research funding is $124 per capita but highest concentrations

23 http://www.pewtrusts.org/en/research-and-analysis/issue-briefs/2015/06/federal-and-state-funding-of-higher-education

tend to be in the Northeast. The national average for Pell Grant funding is $2,078 per full-time equivalent undergraduate student, however states with higher average Pell Grant funding are concentrated in the Southeast.

What can you take away from all these statistics?

Federal funding has largely increased due to increases in Pell Grant programs and Veteran's education benefits. Much of this increase occurred in 2010 after Congress passed the Healthcare and Education Reconciliation Act of 2010 which was estimated to save $68.7 billion by eliminating the FFEL program. This estimated savings was used to increase funding for the Pell Grant program.

State funding has continued to decline by varying amounts per state since 2008. Montana, North Dakota, and Wyoming have actually increased state funding from 2008-2015. Let's take a closer look at my home state of Iowa. Per-student funding for Iowa's public colleges and universities is 22% below 2008 levels while the average tuition has increased by $770.

In Wisconsin the change is even more drastic. Per-student funding for Wisconsin's public colleges is 25% below 2008 levels while the average tuition has increased by $1,485.

I pulled the above statistics from the Center on Budget and Policy Priorities. They have links to each state (minus the three who increased funding) so you can examine the change in higher education funding in your state. I encourage you to check out your state's funding at http://www.cbpp.org/research/state-by-state-fact-sheets-higher-education-cuts-jeopardize-students-and-states-economic

Current Student Loan Related Legislation

So what is going on right now in legislation? Is there anything out there worth learning about? Is there anything out there worth the effort of badgering a politician?

You bet there is.

If you go to congress.gov and search "student loan" you will see over 2000 results in current legislation (2015-2016) and 56 results in executive communication. FYI: executive communication is a message sent to the Senate by the President or other executive branch official. A presidential veto is an example of executive communication.

So of the 2000 plus results in legislation what should you know about?

College for All Act

Introduced by democratic Senator Bernie Sanders (VT) 05/19/15. Read twice and referred to the Committee on Finance. The goal of this plan is to completely eliminate college tuition at four-year public universities. The bill proposed a 67% federal and 33% state split of footing the bill. [24]

This was Senator Sanders' huge platform when he ran for Democratic presidential nominee. According to PredictGov this bill has a 1% chance of being enacted.

The College for All Act was also introduced in the House by democratic representative Alan Grayson (FL) on 01/13/16 and referred to the House Committee on Education and the Workforce, on 03/23/16 it was referred to the Subcommittee on Higher Education and Workforce Training.

Student Loan Repayment Assistance Act

Introduced in the House by democratic representative Scott Peters (CA) 03/26/15 and referred to the House Committee on Ways and Means that same day. The

---

24 https://www.congress.gov/bill/114th-congress/senate-bill/1373/all-info?resultIndex=3

goal of this bill is to modify the IRS code to support employer-matched student loan repayment pre-tax. It would allow an employee to deduct up to $6,000 annually of employer-matched student loan debt payments from their income taxes with a lifetime cap of $50,000. [25]

According to PredictGov the bill has <1% chance of being enacted.

Student Loan Employment Benefits Act of 2016

Introduced in the House by democratic representative Steve Israel (NY) 06/03/2016 and referred to the House Committee on Ways and Means that same day. This bill is very similar to the Student Loan Repayment Assistance Act, the main difference is that it allows for $5,000 of annual amounts paid by an employer under a student loan payment assistance program to be deducted. [26]

According to PredictGov the bill has a 1% chance of being enacted.

---

25 https://www.congress.gov/bill/114th-congress/house-bill/1713/all-info

26 https://www.congress.gov/bill/114th-congress/house-bill/5382/all-info

Higher Ed Act

Introduced in the House by democratic representative Peter DeFazio 09/28/2016 and referred to House Education and the Workforce then referred to House Judiciary on that same day. On 10/19/2016 it was referred to the Subcommittee on Regulatory Reform, Commercial And Antitrust Law. This bill is designed to help improve grants for higher education & repayment of expensive debt. [27]

According to PredictGov this bill has a 1% chance of being enacted.

Creating Higher Education Affordability Necessary to Compete Economically Act or the Middle Class CHANCE Act

Introduced in the House by democratic representative Loretta Sanchez (CA) 05/23/16 and referred to the House Committee on Education and the Workforce that same day and then referred to the Subcommittee on Higher Education and Workforce Training 09/19/16. The intent of this bill is to increase the

---

27 https://www.congress.gov/bill/114th-congress/house-bill/6239/text?q=%7B%22search%22%3A%5B%22student+loans%22%5D%7D&resultIndex=2

maximum Federal Pell Grant award for academic year 2017-2018 and adjust it in subsequent award years to account for changes in the Consumer Price Index. It also restores year-round Pell Grants and increases the semesters of eligibility from 12 to 15. [28]

I don't want to overwhelm you with student loan legislation. These are a just a few examples of what's out there right now.

Two excellent sources for information about student loan legislation include congress.gov where you can search current legislation by topic and govtrack. us which helps track proposed legislation and offers a percentage score of likelihood of bills being enacted.

You may have noticed a surprising trend in the likelihood of these bills being enacted. They're sitting at about 1%. That doesn't seem like a very good chance.

There are thousands of bills that enter congress and the vast majority of them fail. 85% of bills (excluding resolutions) fail in the states every session.

So how can you decide if a bill you actually give a shit about is likely to pass?

---

28 https://www.congress.gov/bill/114th-congress/house-bill/5310

Figure out if it's a hot topic. With the campaign of Senator Bernie Sanders the cost of college education is definitely a hot topic.

Find out who sponsors the bill. If the bill has sponsorship from the majority party or bi-partisan sponsorship it's more likely to succeed than if it was proposed by the minority party.

Research the sponsors of the bill. Do they hold leadership positions or chairmanship? What committees are they involved in?

Is this bill the only possible solution or do multiple competing bills exist? If your topic is a hot topic, like student loan debt, you're likely to find competing bills.

What can you do to up-level the importance of a bill?

Make personal contact with your legislator and talk about the impact a specific bill will have on you. Tell them it's an important issue for you and tell them how you would like them to vote on it (if the bill is up for a vote).

Even though the millennial generation makes up 31% of the electorate vote we don't do a great job voting and taking political action on the issues we care about.

A Facebook rant about how much we're getting screwed doesn't do much good, politics are still pretty old school. Political solutions lie in action outside of social media.

So you want to contact your legislator.

Ok so you've found something that's politically important to you... now what? Who do you even contact, how do you contact them?

To find your senator go to http://www.senate. gov/general/contact_information/senators_cfm. cfm?State=WI and select your state. There will be links in the search results to your state's US senators where you'll find contact information.

To find your representative go to http://www. house.gov/ and search by state. There will be links under your state where you'll find contact information.

What do you say?

If you're contacting your representative by phone you're almost guaranteed to go straight to voice-mail. Be prepared to leave a message that tells them what city you live in, what bill you're calling about, and what you would like them to do. Here's an example script I could use for my Wisconsin senators or representatives.

Hi my name is Jeni Burckart and I'm a registered voter in La Crosse. I wanted to talk to you about the Student Loan Repayment Assistance Act introduced in the House by representative Peters. This act represents an important step for helping Americans with student loan debt.

I graduated in 2013 with my Pharm.D. from an in-state public institution with $128,000 of student loan debt despite working two jobs through college. Work ethic isn't the cause of crushing student loan debt, rising costs are. Proactive change is too late for those of us with debt, we need some legislative help to assist us in digging ourselves out.

The Student Loan Repayment Assistance Act is one piece of legislation that could incentivize employers to offer more loan repayment assistance programs and help ease some of the student loan debt burden.

I would love to talk with you more about this bill. Feel free to call me at (555)555-1234.

Boom, done. Five minutes of your life lead to millennials and people with student loan debt being represented. Look at you exercising your voter power #democracywins

What if you're a little too nervous to make a phone call?

You can try sending an email. You can find your legislators' email addresses in their contact information. Email is much less personal, think about how busy your own inbox gets. But it's still doing something and worth a try.

Your best bet is to keep it short and to the point. The example phone script above works well. Let them know you would be happy to continue the conversation and that they can email you back (bonus points if you ask them to call you).

You can also try tweeting your representative if they have Twitter. You can do a thumbs up or down emoji along with the bill name you're interested in plus any relevant hashtags.

However you decide to get in touch with your legislator be courteous, professional, and tell your story. Help them connect a human being to the bill. Give them someone to picture when they're looking at the impact this bill will have on their constituents.

Don't forget the power the millennial generation holds in this democracy. Thirty-one percent of the electorate is no small number.

It's up to us to infuse that number with power. You're informed about student loan debt history, you know how colleges are funded, you know a few relevant bills, and now you know how to contact your legislator.

You're primed for creating big time change. In this democracy we can push for change to make student loan debt repayable.

Chapter 7

● ● ●

Reliable Sources

It's exhausting when you don't know what to do. You know you need information but for the life of you can't seem to find what you need. This chapter's here to help you sort out the various sources of student loan debt information.

When you're searching for answers you want accurate information, not garbage. Finding the correct information can mean the difference between taking care of business and worrying about what you should do or making a mistake.

Sometimes information can be overwhelming, it's easy to get stuck down a rabbit hole without being any closer to the answer you were searching for.

This chapter will help you find every level of evidence you're looking for no matter how much (or how little) you want to research.

You need to figure out something logistical with your student loans.

Your source: Studentloans.gov

What you'll find: Tools and resources for student loan management. It has things like the direct consolidation loan application, repayment plan information, payment calculators, and information about loan forgiveness. The information you find here can be 100% trusted because it comes straight from the source of your federal loan funding.

How much work it takes: The website is a little cumbersome so it will take some time and digging to find exactly what you want.

Your source: studentaid.ed.gov

What you'll find: You'll find everything from the basics of how to take out loans to repayment and forgiveness options. The information you're likely after is in the How To Repay Your Loans subheading.

How much work it takes: It takes a little bit of digging and a little bit of reading but this website has a pretty functional search tool that works to help you find the information you're after.

You want to figure out how much you owe, find tax forms, or change your repayment plan.

Your source: Your loan servicer website.

What you'll find: It depends on the loan servicer but all of them will have the balance you owe, your current monthly payment and historic payments, tax forms, and information about how to change your repayment plan.

How much work it takes: It's easy to check your balance, find your tax forms, and look at your current and historic monthly payments. It can be a little more arduous to change your repayment plan and might require a phone call or two. Some loan servicers have more helpful customer service than others so the amount of time you'll spend to resolve an issue will vary.

You want to find stats on student loan debt.

<u>Your source</u>: http://nces.ed.gov/programs/digest/current_tables.asp

<u>What you'll find</u>: Statistics about every type of education from kindergarten to graduate school. You're probably most interested in post-secondary education statistics. They have so much information, everything from enrollment to security and crime to financial aid. If you're wondering if something you heard was true, this is a great resource for fact-checking!

<u>How much work it takes</u>: How curious are you? You can spend hours reading these tables and charts... I know I did when I wrote this very book. It's fascinating information but can get overwhelming.

<u>Your source</u>: http://www.pewsocialtrends.org/topics/student-loans/

<u>What you'll find</u>: Descriptive information about student loan debt in word form. The articles will highlight a few key statistics and do the interpreting and describing for you which can be nice. You won't be overwhelmed with data here.

<u>How much work it takes</u>: It depends a little on the depth of your curiosity but in general Pew articles are

easy to digest and quick reads meant to convey the picture data paints.

You want to get a student loan debt knowledge base but you're not sure where to start.

<u>Your sources</u>: repayable.org, facebook.com/1bookvs1trillion/, the book Repayable

<u>What you'll find</u>: If you're searching for baseline student loan debt knowledge but don't really know where to start and don't want to get super-involved and wrapped up in the whole ordeal start with my book Repayable. It does require you to read (or maybe listen if I can get my act together to record an audiobook).

If the idea of reading an entire book is too much for you, go to the Facebook page and ask your question, I'll answer what I can and point you in the right direction for additional information.

If you just want to poke around without getting involved at all, head to repayable.org for shareable student loan debt stats, blog posts, and how to contact your legislator if you want to push for change.

Information about legislation

I dove into legislation last chapter and want to re-list those resources here so you can find everything in one place.

<u>Your source</u>: www.congress.gov

<u>What you'll find</u>: for searchable information by topic and details like summary, bill text, actions, cosponsors, committees, and related bills for each bill currently introduced.

<u>How much work it takes</u>: It's going to take some digging on your part, especially if you're after the details. You can spend hours on this website.

<u>Your source</u>: http://www.senate.gov/general/contact_ information/senators_cfm.cfm?State=WI (senators) and http://www.house.gov/ (representatives)

<u>What you'll find</u>: Contact information for representatives/senators. Most will have links to their websites, phone numbers, email addresses, mailing addresses.

<u>How much work it takes</u>: Finding the information won't take much work a quick search will get you to contact information in less than a minute. The real work comes in when you decide to actually reach out

to that person. That can take anywhere from 5 minutes to leave a message or longer if you actually speak to a human being.

What about general big-picture life questions?

You want to know how to make student loan debt fit into your life, not fit your life into your student loan debt. There's not any one particular source of information that does a great job telling you how to buy a house or save for retirement when you have student loan debt.

Since you've trusted me enough to read this far in the book let me give you my best advice for each of these scenarios. There are no hard and fast rules or black and white answers, more like 50 shades of gray. That's why this is just my best advice and it isn't guaranteed to work for your financial situation.

How to repay your debt and save for retirement

Let's start by breaking down the existing retirement options. You have employer-sponsored plans aka 401Ks and then you have individual contribution plans aka IRA's. Each of these options comes in two flavors: traditional and Roth.

Contributions to a traditional 401K or IRA are made pre-tax so they are deducted from your taxable income and then taxed when you withdraw them (typically in retirement). Contributions made to Roth 401Ks or IRAs are made after taxes have been taken out of your paycheck. That means they don't decrease your taxable income and that they won't be taxed when you collect on them in retirement.

Which type of retirement plan you choose is up to you. I've chosen to contribute to a Roth 401K so my taxes are taken out now. This is based on my plan to have many other income streams and investments leading to a higher taxable income in the future.

Many people will choose a traditional 401K because they presume that on retirement they will have a lower taxable income than they do today. The type of plan you choose depends on your outlook for the future.

Conventional wisdom tells you to contribute everything you can to retirement to maximize compounding interest. Money contributed early on makes you more money in interest than money contributed later on. The problem is, your student loan debt has compounding interest too...

So what's the smart strategy for repaying debt that's earning you an interest rate of 6.8% without bankrupting your future self?

If you have an employer-matched 401K you absolutely need to contribute something, even if you can only afford to contribute 1% of your annual income. Employer money is free money and this helps you get some of that money while building the habit of saving for retirement.

If you can afford to make more than your required monthly student loan payments, contribute up to the max amount your employer will match. Why? So you can get all that free money they're giving you. You'll get somewhere around an 80% return rate from your employer match for those contributions which is way above the interest rate on your student loans.

Why not contribute anything above the employer match? Your student loan debt is guaranteed to earn you 6.8% interest and your 401K contribution isn't guaranteed to have a positive return. If you still have extra money to delegate after getting the max employer match my advice is to put it toward your student loans.

My advice is to continue this strategy until you've repaid your student loan debt.

How to save for home while repaying student loan debt

The decision to rent or buy while you have student loan debt is largely a personal decision. It depends on how you view each of these two living arrangements, your income, the price of homes in the market, and the cost of rent in your area.

Buying a home can protect you from rising rent prices, provide a sort of savings plan by building your equity, and generally the value of the home appreciates over time (though don't forget about 2008's housing crash). The intangible benefit of having a place that you own can't be discounted either.

However most financial advisors will caution you against considering a home as an "investment". In general property taxes, maintenance, and insurance are all lost income that's not recovered when you sell.

You also have the high cost of buying and selling your home to consider.

Renting can actually be the smarter financial option depending on your income, the price of the home, the amount you're paying for rent now, and how long you want to stay.

One of the biggest factors in determining if you should rent or buy is how long you plan to stay in your house. If you plan to stay for at least five to seven years and probably longer, buying will likely make more sense.

Your best resource for estimating the financial impact of buying vs. renting is this handy calculator from the New York Times (Google New York Times rent vs buy or find it here http://www.nytimes.com/interactive/2014/upshot/buy-rent-calculator.html?_r=0). The estimator has multiple sliders so you can estimate your personal benefit based on your actual finances!

So if you've decided to save up and buy a house how do you do it with your student loan debt?

First of all you need to find as high of interest earning savings account as possible. Some banks and credit unions offer first time home buyers savings accounts that earn 1.5% or more. Remember, you're diverting money from debt that's sitting at 6.8% interest so it's worth your time to hunt for a good rate.

My advice is to put off buying and saving for a house until your debt is repaid. Financially you will be better served by repaying that high-interest debt.

Unless you're in an income-based repayment plan and expecting loan forgiveness after 10 years. If that's you, you might have a significant amount of money left over after your required monthly payments so you could save it all for a home without delaying your timeline for repayment.

The advice I've offered about retirement and home spending is just that, advice. You have to explore the details of your financial situation to understand what decisions are best for you.

There are many different beliefs circulating about how best to build wealth while living your life and you may subscribe to a different view than mine.

These are just bullet points for exploration of big financial ideas. Use this information as a starting point for making responsible financial decisions.

When it comes to student loan debt, knowledge is power. If you've ever wondered about something, look it up. If you find an interesting or surprising statistic please be sure to share on the Repayable Facebook page.

Using accurate and reliable information is the key to building a strong case for change. Research to your heart's content!

Chapter 8

● ● ●

Dominate Your Debt

This chapter is here to give you realistic action steps you can take so you can repay your student loans in a reasonable amount of time. It's not some garbage *don't buy a coffee ever again* advice.

This advice is all about being smart with your money so you can still spend on what you love while repaying your debt. Besides, if skipping coffees was the secret we'd all be out of debt by now.

This chapter will help you measure the cost of these suggestions against the benefits of repaying your student loans. Think about finally paying off your loans and starting your own business, traveling, buying a house, or changing careers. Now read on and get ready to work.

None of the advice in this chapter is some miraculous secret. The most helpful advice is about making small changes. It will all require *you* to do something. The chapter isn't called *Disappear Your Debt* because there's no magic bullet for making student loan debt vanish.

The most important thing you can do is truly own your debt. Know your number and keep that amount fresh in your brain.

If you ever want to make your student loan debt truly repayable you're going to have to own your number. I've noticed an odd trend in people repaying student loan debt.

We won't fully recognize our actual debt amount. I hear folks saying things like *I have about 50K in student loan debt.* When I ask further exactly how much they truly don't know. I mean, you're sacrificing a sizeable chunk of your income every month to repay your debt.

So why the hell don't people know exactly how much they owe?!

It's a form of grief, seriously, it's denial. Like if you don't cognitively acknowledge your exact burden of debt it's not real. Sorry but acknowledge it or not, it's real.

Step 1 For Debt Domination: Go to your student loan servicer right now and look at your total debt amount. Say it out loud *"I owe _____ ($89,568) in student loans."*

Alright, fuck that's a lot of money and you might be feeling a bit short of breath but it's fine. You can't defeat something you don't know, so there it is. You know it, you own it, and you're coming for it.

If you're thinking about continuing school or going back to school for an additional degree here are some ways to make the debt domination a little bit easier. If you're done borrowing money and working entirely on repayment you can skip this section and pick back up in the next section.

Reduce the amount you borrow.

Simple advice, and many ways to do it. You still may end up with a ton of debt but even saving yourself

$3-10K over the duration will make your life better on the back end.

The first way is to get scholarships, be sure to apply for anything you might possibly qualify for. It's a lot of work but you can dedicate one day of one weekend to it. There's not a whole lot most people can do for 8 hours that might earn them thousands of dollars.

The second way is to work in college. Do whatever you can. If that's 4 hours a week that's fine. The goal of working is to be able to borrow less to cover living expenses. Unless you're already a professional you probably aren't going to earn a ton of money. But even if you earn enough to cover your rent and groceries for the month you've saved yourself thousands of dollars in debt a year.

The third way is to not borrow the full amount offered to you each year/semester. For example your tuition may cost $4.5K/semester, books may be an additional $500 so you're looking at $5K for the semester. When you get your financial aid package notification they will offer you more than that. They'll probably offer you an additional $3-5K that semester for living expenses.

DON'T TAKE THE EXTRA MONEY. So many people (myself included) rationalize it as a responsible thing to do.

Well I'll take it just in case I need it. I don't really have much of a savings account, and I can always return the money.

Newsflash, you will never return the money and you earned a ton of interest on it.

Also, a piece of information that the financial aid office doesn't widely circulate: if you give the money back at the beginning of the semester you can get it back mid-semester if you need it. It's your money to borrow so if you need access to it you can get it.

I know you can get your money because that happened to me. My final year of pharmacy school I ended up in the hospital and required multiple same-day procedures. Unfortunately these visits spanned November-January which meant I had to pay two deductibles. Being a healthy young individual I had a high-deductible health insurance plan and had to come up with $5000 total for both years' deductibles.

Gulp I did not have $5K lying around. I had returned $10K of loan money because I'd gotten a $10K scholarship that year. I was able to contact my financial aid office and get the additional funding I needed to pay the deductibles.

What about paying on student loan interest while in college?

My best advice again is going to be to borrow less. If you can afford to make any sort of payment on your student loans while you're actively borrowing them you can afford to borrow less.

Choose a degree that pays.

I wrote a whole chapter about the best/worst degrees for your financial sanity. So I won't belabor this point. The single best way you can ensure you can repay your loans comfortably and in a reasonable amount of time is to optimize your debt:income ratio. You can do this through minimizing debt and maximizing income. So picking a degree that has high job placement rates and good income in comparison to the amount you have to borrow is the way to go.

Most of you reading this are probably done borrowing money. So what do you do when you've sealed your fate on the degree front and now you're battling the payments?

Don't take advantage of 6 month deferment period.

If you're employed in any capacity and able to make your student loan payments do so. Don't defer. Your loans still accrue interest the entire six month period which can be thousands of dollars. Even if you can keep up with just interest do that.

If you can't afford the payments in your repayment plan of choice because you're not yet employed in your chosen field, switch to an income-based repayment plan. This plan will allow you to make monthly payments you can afford while helping you make some progress on your student loans.

I can hear your protests now, *Jeni a few hundred bucks just doesn't matter in the scheme of things. I'd be happier keeping that money every month so I can do something fun with it.*

Would you be happier? What are you going to use the money for? Something that really does contribute to your happiness like travel? Or are you going to just piddle it away here and there on stuff you can't even remember?

If it's the latter then make sacrifice and make the payments. It will be so much better for your long term happiness, when the burden of student loan debt looms over you for 6 months less.

Pay extra on top of your required monthly payment when you can, regardless of payment plan.

*Caveat; don't do this if you're in a loan forgiveness program.

Whatever payment plan you're in, you can shorten the time to student loan freedom greatly by making extra payments every month.

A good way to do this is to pay a little on your loans as often as you get paid. So if you get paid bi-monthly you would make two payments on your student loan. One of the payments is your required monthly payment. If you have extra money at that check feel free to add it on to your required payment. Then with your second check make a second payment. Whatever extra you can afford. If it's $20 or $1200 it will make a difference.

*Be sure to discuss how your extra payments are applied with your loan servicer. It's absolutely imperative that your extra payments are applied to principal not to interest. By paying down your principal you decrease the amount of interest your loans earn. This can save you hundreds or thousands in the long term. Applying extra payments to principal only is a financial move that's simple, smart, and literally requires no extra sacrifice on your part.

As a side note not all loan servicers calculate your interest on a monthly basis. For example I refinanced through Earnest and they continuously calculate interest. So whenever I make a payment I pay the interest that has accrued since I last made a payment.

So my extra payments aren't 100% applied to principle, but it also means that my monthly required payment has less interest because I already paid some interest.

This is a slight disadvantage for the borrower but TBH I still saved >$10K in interest by halving my interest rate so I'm way ahead.

Set up as aggressive of a payment plan as makes sense for you.

This goes against almost all financial advice I've ever read. Your student loan debt is not doing you any favors by lingering around like a bad fart. Clear the air as quickly as possible.

To do this you need to set up an aggressive repayment plan. Conventional wisdom says set yourself up with as much cushion as possible so you don't get yourself into financial trouble. You can always make extra payments when you have the extra funds.

Yes, you can always pay extra but will you? Will you really pay extra on student loans when you could buy so many extra incubators for Pokémon Go?

The key is to find an appropriate balance. You want to be able to spend on things that make you happy, like hanging out with friends. You also really want to get rid of your debt. Look at your overall financial picture.

Do you have <3 months in an emergency savings account? Red light, no extra payments or payment plans too aggressive to allow savings for you. Do you have 3 months of savings in an emergency account? If so you get a yellow light proceed with aggressive payments cautiously. Do you have six months of savings? You've got a green light, go for the aggressive payments.

If you decide to refinance your student loans some companies allow you ultimate flexibility in determining your monthly payment. For example Earnest has a slider that helps you determine interest rates based on monthly payments. You can also see the term of your loan change either increasing or decreasing the lower or higher your monthly payment.

Earnest will also let you update your monthly payment amount without a ton of hassle. This means if you thought you could afford $1500/month but it's stretching you too thin you can decrease the payment. Or if you were pretty sure you would pay the extra and wanted flexibility but find you're wasting your extra money you can increase your payment.

The most aggressive you can get with a payment plan through a federal loan servicer is typically the 10 year repayment plan.

Your Debt is Not a Tax Break

Ok it might be, but it's not a good reason to keep it hanging around. If you make over $80K annually as an individual or >$120K annually as a married couple you can't deduct the interest you've paid on your student loan debt. So it's literally worthless for anyone in those income groups.

What if you make less than that though? How much is a student loan debt interest deduction really worth?

I'll use a few generalizations to describe the "value" of deducting student loan debt interest.

The US has three tax brackets under the $80K and $120K cutoffs. People in different brackets are taxed at different rates. The less money you make the lower the percentage of taxes you have to pay.

2016 Taxable Income Brackets and Rates (Estimate)		
Rate	Single Filers	Married Joint Filers
10%	$0 to $9,275	$0 to $18,550
15%	$9,275 to $37,650	$18,550 to $75,300
25%	$37,650 to $91,150	$75,300 to $151,900

http://taxfoundation.org/article/2016-tax-brackets

So will deducting your student loan interest put you in a different tax bracket? Maybe. Check out the table above (subtract your interest amount from your total income).

Another reason the student loan interest deduction isn't as good as you think it is; according to the federal tax code you can only deduct $2500 from your taxable income. So the government will owe you the taxes you paid on that $2500. Is $2500 enough to move you into a lower tax bracket? Probably not. It might be if you combine it with other deductions like 401K contributions.

Keeping debt around solely for a tax deduction is stupid. With interest rates near 7% it doesn't add up financially. You will pay more in interest than you will get back in taxes. Unless the government just gives you the $2500 back or you move tax brackets you didn't keep more of your money by hanging onto your debt.

If you're in that higher income range you'll pay $14K in interest and not get a dime back... Never mind the fact that you had to take out all that student loan debt to earn the income to be in that tax bracket. You're still middle class and the government is happy to double dip and take your interest and your taxes.

Set a Realistic Budget Based on Your Lifestyle

Do you love to travel? Work on a side hustle? Have a fabulous wardrobe? Season tickets to watch Hawkeye football? Whatever your most meaningful spending category is find a way to put it in your budget.

Don't completely eliminate spending on something that makes you happy to repay your student loans more quickly. That almost certainly ensures failure when you binge spend because you're miserable.

A reasonable budget includes your required expenses like rent, groceries, other debt payments (mortgage, car loan), utilities, gas, health care, pet care. It also needs to include things that you really want for your mental health like a gym membership and a funding budget for your side hustle so you can pay for your web domain and hosting.

The key to making a budget that works for you is deciding what you spend money on that brings you true enjoyment and then ranking those things. You have to figure out which things matter most and hang on to those then be relentless in the slashing of other expenses.

For me I don't want to spend a ton a rent. I live in an old 60's house that has spiders (which are actually terrifying) but I save $400-600 a month in rent by doing it. It's a safe quiet location and I don't care much about the curb appeal. That's $400-600 a month that I have to either go to student loan debt or to travel or clothing which are both things I love to spend on.

Don't guilt yourself about spending on categories you love. Spend the money and truly enjoy the experience. It will make it worth slashing spending for the less loved categories (like drinking).

The actual mechanics of budgeting are simple and there are a variety of tools available today. My favorite is the Mint app from Intuit. The app lets you connect all your accounts (savings, checking, credit cards, student loans, car loans, retirement accounts) to give you a true picture of your financial wealth.

I look at Mint almost daily to check on my transactions and side-eye my student loans. It's a low-maintenance way to maintain an up to date understanding of your financial status.

For more guidance check out my budgeting post on the Millennial Maxims blog Create a Budget (www.millennialmaxims.com/archives/51).

Refinance or Figure out Loan Forgiveness

I recognize that for some of you this chapter might be full of a little advice a lot too late. Maybe you have massive amounts of loan debt for a degree that just doesn't pay. If this is the case you need to be sure to talk to you loan servicer. DO NOT DEFAULT. Your loan servicer can help you find a realistic payment plan. If you default on your loans you may never qualify for forgiveness or refinancing.

Refinancing is best suited for folks who have a pretty optimal debt:income ratio and tends to favor borrowers with high incomes like pharmacists, physicians, lawyers, etc. You should still try to refinance because even a 1% interest rate decrease is still a savings.

See Chapter 04 Reconsider Your Interest Rates and Chapter 05 Please Forgive Them for details on refinancing and loan forgiveness.

Keep Track of Your Loan Amount and Share and Celebrate Milestones

Making your student loans repayable requires a certain mindset and some motivation. Tracking your progress on your repayments can be incredibly motivating, yea the overall loan amount may still be high but even watching it decrease incrementally can be so rewarding.

When you hit milestones be sure to share it with people. When I finally got under $100K I shared it on Facebook. I think it embarrassed some people but anyone with student debt of their own loved it.

It's a massive accomplishment to repay tens of thousands of dollars. You don't need to share it on Facebook but let your friends know and celebrate by doing something fun!

What about me?

I can hear your wheels turning dear reader. You're thinking *Jeni this stuff works for you because you make six figures. I make $50K how is this going to work for me?*

It's all about debt:income ratio. You need to establish a rate of repayment that's slightly uncomfortable but still allows you to live your life. This might mean it takes longer for you to repay. The other option (my personal favorite) is to start bringing in additional sources of income via a side hustle.

You're stuck with your total debt amount, the Dept of Ed isn't going to magically forget to make you pay your loans or accidentally zero it out (sorry to crush your dreams). There are a few things you can do with that total debt amount like refinancing and applying any extra payments to principal that help you get the most out of your money but ultimately this side of the ratio is somewhat inflexible.

Increase the income side of the ratio.

Find a way to make a little extra money from something you love. It doesn't have to be a ton, any amount helps. If you have the right mindset, income isn't a fixed number that depends on getting a raise from your boss.

It may seem bizarre to you to think about starting something on the side. The fact of the matter is if you make no changes you will see no change in your income.

So how does a person start making extra money?

There are the traditional options of getting a second job, doing odd jobs for people, anything to make a few extra bucks. You can google "ways to make extra money" and find a laundry list of ideas.

But what about starting a side hustle? Well, it's going to take a lot of extra work, working on things on your days off, working on things before and after work.

To make it successful you need to pick something you're passionate about, something that you're perpetually curious about, and some problem that doesn't have quite the right solution. When you find that thing you're going to have to develop that solution. Not the one you think it needs but the one that people actually want.

There are so many books and podcasts about how to start a business. You need to do the research yourself to decide if this is right for you.

Here are my top resources to get you started. I have read each of these books and listened to each of these podcasts.

Books: *Will it Fly?* Pat Flynn
    One Simple Idea Stephen Key
    The E-Myth Revisited Michael Gerber
Podcasts: *Smart Passive Income* Pat Flynn
    EOFire (Entrepreneur on Fire) John Lee Dumas
    Solopreneur Hour Michael O'Neil

You have control over what you do in your free time, write a book on something you're passionate about, start a blog, sell some of your old stuff on ebay or craigslist, pick up freelancing work on Upwork. The internet makes the possibilities endless.

You're accountable for your financial future and student loan debt doesn't have to stop you from having a successful one.

Chapter 9

● ● ●

A New Hope

I want to paint a different picture for student loan debt. I want to paint a picture of hope and opportunity. Student loan debt sucks, there's no doubt about it. Dwelling on the negatives and the burden of student loan debt does nothing to make it go away. A positive focus opens your mind to possibilities, to creative thinking that could contain the new way of educating or funding education that eliminates the burden.

This chapter is here to give you a few ideas of where our millennial generation could start a movement. It gives you a problem-solving mindset so you can create the innovation that relieves your specific burden. Who better to develop the solution than those of us most pained by the problem?

You can advocate for your needs rather than relying on someone without firsthand knowledge to do it for you. You can develop solutions that actually serve and meet the needs of the indebted.

You can create change for future college graduates and live up to our generation's socially conscious reputation by preventing future graduates from suffering an ever-increasing burden.

You can change the course of the history of education. Prevent education from becoming limited to only the wealthiest Americans and keep student loan debt from widening the wealth gap.

It's up to you and it's a big responsibility. This is something all of your millennial life experience can change. You have the ambition, the firsthand experience, the pain, the education, and the need to do something bigger than yourself.

You have what it takes to be a voice in our movement. The movement that crushes student loan debt.

I can hear your doubts. You're saying *Jeni none of my hopes and dreams matter because this is way too big a problem to solve.*

Not true, with Senator Bernie Sanders' rise to the presidential candidate election stage the cost of college is a hot topic of discussion at the national level. There is no better time than now.

Millennials are the largest living generation in the US, it's time to use our numbers to look out for our interests and those of future college grads.

Fine you say *I push for change, say it finally happens. Who's to say it doesn't just get reversed when political parties change or when education and financing lobbyists start to holler?*

No one can know what the future holds. But by continually advocating, talking about, and most importantly voting on issues related to student loan debt you can push change. Remember how big our generation is, in a democracy this still matters if we show up to vote!

Are you ready to read on and get your wheels turning? Ready to spark some student loan activism? Let's do this!

How Colleges Can Shape the Future of Student Loan Debt

Colleges can publish average student loan debt load, job placement rates, and average incomes for all individuals who graduate with a specific degree. Included in these figures should be all outliers including the highest and lowest of the average and a description of whether the data were normally distributed or not.

This information should be supplied and readily available on the college website within information about every single degree. In addition these statistics should be a part of admissions counseling.

Why this helps: These data give an accurate picture of the true cost of obtaining a specific degree and allow individuals to determine their long term financial outcomes. The additional statistics about outliers and distribution of data point out whether or not the data paint an accurate picture or were skewed by a few high or low earners.

College need to take responsibility for their funding and tuition and be held accountable to students. The stat I'm about to share is painful and I wish it wasn't true but it is. Please don't interpret this as me saying that we should cut funding for colleges. No need to Hulk out and stop reading.

Brace yourself.

A Federal Reserve Bank of New York Staff Reports released in July of 2015 and revised in March of 2016 drew the following conclusion:

"In this paper, we use a Bartik-like approach to identify the effect of increased loan supply on tuition following large policy changes in federal aid program maximums available to undergraduate students that occurred between 2008 and 2010....**We find that institutions that were most exposed to these maximums ahead of the policy changes experienced disproportionate tuition increases around these changes**, with effects of changes in institution-specific program maximums of Pell Grant, subsidized loan, and unsubsidized loan of about 40, 60, and 15 cents on the dollar, respectively.."

There is a ton of interesting information in this report and it comes out at about 60 pages but a lot of it is references and graphs. There's probably only about 30 pages of written material. If you want to dig deep

into it I encourage you to check it out. https://www.
newyorkfed.org/medialibrary/media/research/staff_
reports/sr733.pdf

All of this is saying that colleges have a role and
responsibility to their students to keep tuition costs
reasonable and not insatiably gobble up new funding.
That role is very tricky for me to define.

I don't know the inner workings of college budgets
and don't claim to. I would think that a few things
could help improve their fiscal responsibility and one
of them would be large scale information transparency. Public institutions already have some of this information available.

When a buyer gets to see the business practices
of a company they either like it or don't and can use
that to choose to do business elsewhere. From an education standpoint I think it would be similar. The
supply of colleges with quality educations is high.
The best college candidates will get into the schools
they want to go to. The very act of being transparent helps encourage an ethical and responsible fiscal
environment.

How Government Can Shape the Future of Student Loan Debt

My suggestions are going to involve regulation. It's what our government does best or worst depending on your perspective. Public education is already state and federally funded so perhaps more regulation of how these funds are applied really does make sense. Public universities have governing boards (the name depends on the state), in IA, WI, and MN the governing body is the board of regents. These boards may contain members appointed by the state governor.

There is already a lot of oversight for public universities so perhaps we could give that oversight more direction.

Here are some of the directions I think it might be interesting to flesh out and explore further.

Could annual tuition increases be regulated? This would likely need to be done in conjunction with not hacking state funding for these institutions. It seems like cutting funding for higher education is like finding money in the couch to policy makers. *Oooh I found a few million dollars… and an M&M!*

I'm thinking something along the lines of a rent cap or rent stabilization. Similar to how rent controlled properties work in NYC. The idea is that you don't squeeze folks less able to afford renting, or in this case tuition, out of the market.

So for example if there was a tuition cap the government would say, if you start a 4 year degree program in 2016 at an annual tuition of $8000 you will continue to pay only $8000 annually until you graduate. There should probably be some kind of time limit and enrollment status requirement to encourage graduation in a timely manner.

A possible problem I could see with this is that essentially for each new class colleges would charge more and more tuition because they would know they couldn't increase it for those students for 6-8 years (or whatever the term).

Another way the government can shape the future of student loan debt is to hold the interest rates low. Student loan interest rates are not reflective of current market value and they don't get updated to reflect market value.

This lack of response to market interest rates can be seen as an advantage. If there's high inflation it means student loan interest rates will take longer to respond and hopefully don't incur the same sharp increases as say a mortgage interest rate would.

The downside to this though is that when interest rates are low (like right now) you're paying well above standard amounts and that's a difference of thousands of dollars.

The government could make student loan interest rates more reflective of the financial market.

I think the better option is simply to standardize the interest rates around 2%. I understand that in years of inflation the government could lose money. If there are a lot of students who default on their loan repayment then the government could lose money.

As interest rates exist currently the government typically loses money on funding student loans. It might be shocking to hear that considering how high the interest rates seem to be. It also depends on which calculation you use. I tend to believe the estimates of the Congressional Budget Office which uses a more conservative formula. This conservative formula predicts losses.

However, unlike regular creditors, federal student loans aren't based on any type of credit-worthiness or ability to pay. This is a good thing because not many 18 year olds have credit and it keeps education accessible regardless of socioeconomic status.

Where this is all pointing is that the exponential growth in the cost of a college education needs to be curtailed. This would help minimize the risks of defaulting and losing money due to inflation.

Lastly there is an option to make a college education at a public university free or incredibly low-cost. With Senator Bernie Sanders making it to the democratic presidential candidate stage we finally had a politician who truly seemed to grasp the impact student loan debt is having on the future of this country.

He proposed a plan that would have provided free public college education for the masses. I think this is a lofty goal and something that could be done. Remember when healthcare wasn't universal? Yea that plan has had it's share of bumps and shortcomings but I think it has shifted the conversation surrounding healthcare.

We can shift the conversation surrounding college education too. We need to find and vote for individuals who understand the needs of our generation and make policy change to help meet those needs.

*Free education is great and all but I already have my
student loan debt so now what? Do I just pay more taxes
so someone else gets the benefit while I drown in my debt?*

I hear you on this one as I share the exact same
sentiment. I think it is key that as a generation we
develop a consistent message that closely looks at the
impact on all student loan borrowers. We don't want
to benefit a few folks at one stage of the education
pipeline to the detriment of others at a different stage
in the pipeline.

A strategic and well-rounded approach is needed
for maximal benefit. If we truly want strategy sessions
and government time to be devoted to this we will
need to vote and make our voices heard.

We need to propose solutions, we need to make
it easier for people who don't share our perspective to
understand our situation. We need to make solutions
known that would actually be helpful to us rather
than relying on someone else to think of it.

In the resources on www.repayable.org you will
find links to find the members of congress for your
state along with their contact information. You will
also find a script you can use to make a phone call to
this congress member to advocate for future change.

Call them and share your idea, give them your contact information and let them know you would like to hear back from them. Make it as easy as possible for them to contact you. Be persistent. Don't stop making your voice heard. If we got our entire generation to do that our congress would be so annoyed with us they'd have to devote some time to solving this problem ☺

You can also find social media information for your members of congress and post your ideas on their Facebook page or tweet at them.

An example tweet would look like this "@ SenatorBaldwin we need student loan debt reform WI graduates have an avg of >$28K in student loan debt! #repayable #EducationForAll"

Employer Opportunities for Student Loan Repayment Assistance

There are a few employer sponsored student loan repayment options out there. Employers will match an employee's student loan debt contributions up to a certain dollar amount of student loan debt repayment.

So for example an employer will match up $1200 per year in student loan debt payments. That means your $1200 paid toward your debt doubled to $2400 in repayment.

If the tax exempt options were the same as 401K we would really be onto something. Imagine if like a 401K you could contribute $18000 of pre-tax money to your student loans. Essentially decreasing your taxable income.

Imagine if instead of matching a certain dollar amount your employer matched a percentage of your income (like with 401K), you could get an employer match of 5% of your income contributed to your student loan debt, effectively doubling your contributions.

If you could contribute that money pre-tax too like retirement contributions can be made, that'd be solid. I would love to have knocked $18k out of the $30K I paid on my loans off my income last year. But instead I couldn't even deduct any of the money I paid in interest on my student loans.

Other employer opportunities involve contributing a certain dollar amount toward education. A lot of employees use this to obtain advanced degrees.

Essentially this is an incredibly effective way to eliminate the burden of debt right away up front.

You don't have to borrow as much (if any) money so you don't accrue the debt and the interest like you do when you self-fund your education.

Some employers simply educate you on the job. This is more common in technical type jobs but again it's effective in eliminating the need for debt at all.

Crowdfunding Student Loan Debt Repayment

Essentially this idea is stolen from Camille Perri's book *The Assistants* in which a group of underpaid assistants working for a multimillion dollar company starts stealing money to repay student loans.

Obviously I'm not advocating for stealing. Later in the book they start collecting donations to start a non-profit which collects donations for student loan repayment.

Essentially it's like crowd-funding student loan repayment. In the book the recipients of the donated money are chosen at random.

I can hear your thoughts now. *Why would anyone donate to repaying student loans?*

My question back is *Why not?*

The Millennial generation is the largest living generation in this country. Fiscal decisions that help us will help drive future economics and investing.

This is my vision for crowd-funding student loan debt: Essentially a person would set up a non-profit organization. Ideally this would be started in a way that could build buzz for the endeavor. I'm thinking something like using a Kickstarter or Indiegogo campaign.

The crowd-funding campaign would only be used to get the actual non-profit off the ground and running. The participation of hopefully thousands or tens of thousands of millennials would highlight the interest and importance of student loan debt.

When corporate donors recognized the importance of this cause to the largest living generation the goodness of their hearts (i.e. the opportunity to snag a generation's buying loyalty) would motivate them to donate large sums of money.

Like all nonprofits money can be made by small donations from massive number of donors or by massive donations made by a small number of donors.

Imagine getting big companies like Microsoft and Apple (millennial-focused companies) to pitch a significant chunk of their donated funds to this cause.

At the same time a generation of 84 million individuals donating even $10 would be $840 million available to repay the $1.3 trillion in student loan debt. This isn't a non-significant dent either.

So how would the money be distributed? Who would get it? Would it be determined by need? How would anyone know the impact it would make?

Taking a page straight from *The Assistants* I think a random lottery would be the best way to distribute the funds. It would be important to pay off both low dollar amounts and high dollar amounts.

The money would be distributed in the total amount required to entirely repay someone's remaining student loan debt. So yes this means some recipients would receive more money than others. The goal is not to create equality in terms of dollar amount received but to create a playing field where our generation starts adult life without massive amounts of debt.

It's difficult to say if there should be need-based restrictions on the distribution of funds. What if someone's parents can just repay their loan amount?

Should the non-profit really be giving them the money when someone else can barely afford their monthly payments?

The ethical questions surrounding the non-profit are quite involved and would take a lot of deciding. Ultimately I would be in favor of some sort of restriction but it would be very generous. It wouldn't necessarily be income-based but might be debt:income ratio based.

One of the requirements of receiving student loan repayment from the non-profit would be that each recipient would share the impact on their life of no longer having debt. People could share it in a video or an email.

This would help connect donors to the cause and help us be sure there was still a need for the non-profit to continue. In the end the goal of the non-profit would be to put ourselves out of work.

If student loan debt reform involved colleges controlling tuition hikes and having solid financial aid education, the government regulating interest rates and establishing policies for lower-cost public education, employers beefing up repayment options and education incentives, personal fiscal responsibility, and possibly a non-profit with funding for those already stuck with student loan debt, we could eliminate the burden of student loan debt.

Our generation with the help of colleges, employers, policymakers, and our own resourcefulness and relentless pursuit of reform could make this book useless!

Seriously I would love to work myself out of this passion. If we could implement widespread change and shift public perception of student loan debt we could beat this thing. One book vs. $1.3 trillion in student loan debt. You've got this!

I want to hear your pipe dreams and crazy ideas for solving student loan debt. Whatever it is I want to hear it. I mean let's get real; one of my favorite ideas is based on a fictional book and involves crowd-funding student loan repayment ☺

One thing I know for sure is this "If you never try, you'll never know".

Chapter 10

● ● ●

Make it Viral

The goal of this book is to start a movement. I refuse to let my generation limp away to a dark place of financial disaster where we're crippled by student loan debt and feel nothing can be done.

But the thing is, I'm only one voice. One loud, outspoken, relentless voice, but still only one voice. I need you dear reader to talk about student loan debt. I need to you to share your personal experience. I need you to educate the future generation and even your fellow college grads.

People connect with people. They don't connect with statistics. They don't connect with one millennial author writing a 30,000 word book on the subject. They connect with you, with your face, your experience, and your reality. Because you connect with them.

The more people who share their story the more likely it is that someone will see themselves reflected. That they will get a glimpse at their future and make the best decisions they can. That they will have applicable information to guide them.

I can hear your thoughts (isn't it annoying that I'm also a mind-reader). *Jeni, don't you think discussing income and debt is petty? I mean if you make six figures and you're complaining about the impact your debt has on you to someone who makes $50K, isn't that offensive?*

Socially, it may be a little offensive. It's important to change the social implications of talking money. Just like not discussing wages contributes to gender and racial discrepancies in pay and a sense of shame for those being paid less, not talking debt:income leads to poorly informed borrowing decisions, shame, and lost money.

If you're really uncomfortable about it only discuss debt with people in the same position and pay scale as you.

If you truly don't want to share your financial information that's up to you. I'm not saying you've got to put in on blast and tweet it out or write a book about it. I'm saying that when you're discussing debt with close friends you should be honest.

"An eccentricity made a regular thing of ceases to provoke remark."
– Sylvia Townsend Warner, "Winged Creatures" in Kingdoms of Elfin

Essentially the more you talk about something the more you remove the social stigma and the more "normal" a topic of conversation it becomes.

Ok, Okay you've badgered me to death and I believe it's important to talk about my debt. I'm a little uncomfortable and haven't done this much, where do I start?

That's the way! Here are a few ways to start sharing your story.

Commiserate

Start talking about how expensive it is to go to college. Talk about the common pain points; high interest rates, never-ending payments, people who deny that student loan debt is a real issue, the list is practically never-ending.

While I don't suggest all you do is complain (especially now that you've read an entire book with steps to solve the problem) I do think commiserating sets a non-threatening tone.

When you admit to having a problem or a struggle you free the other person up to admit a struggle of their own. In that moment you've created comradery and safe environment to talk about a sensitive subject.

Dream of the Future

Talk about your hopes for the future. This can easily spawn from the commiseration step. When you're complaining you could say what you would like things to look like instead. i.e. I'm so sick of paying 6.7% interest on my student loan debt, wouldn't it be so much better if interest rates were capped at two percent?

Ask your friends if they could change one thing about student loan debt what would they change?

The answers people give are often surprisingly similar. We have a few fairly recurrent themes within the education system that make student loan debt particularly bothersome.

Get real

Discuss your real student loan debt amount. Instead of saying *I have six figures of debt* say *I have $132,856 in student loan debt.* Vague numbers have an oddly disarming quality about them. Like somehow if you don't announce exactly what you owe it doesn't quite seem real. It seems like a figurative amount of money.

Disclosing the exact amount will have benefits for you too. It's helpful to own your number. It gives you a sense of responsibility and empowerment. Rather than hiding from your debt you're confronting it and taking charge of it.

Be sure to tell them the story of your debt. How many years did you go to school? What degree did you graduate with? Did you identify any missed opportunities to save money? Or did you find a particularly helpful way to reduce your debt?

Depending on your relationship with the person you're talking to you may be comfortable disclosing even more information. If you have a close relationship you should talk about the payment plan you chose and how much that monthly payment is. It could also be helpful to share the impact that payment has on your monthly finances, is it a stretch, do you feel OK, you can afford to pay extra if you want, or does it feel unmanageable?

Providing a realistic example can help others imagine how they can structure their repayment. It can also help them identify repayment strategies that they want to avoid.

Ask them to tell their student loan debt story

If you're comfortable with this person and have a good conversation going around student loan debt give them the opportunity to share their story. It can be cathartic to share your debt scenario with someone who understands where you're coming from.

Ask them how much their education cost them? What payment plan did they choose? When do they expect to pay their debt off?

All this is for the sake of information spreading and sharing. The goal is that a little bit of transparency eliminates the unconscious shame that comes with having huge amounts of debt. It's also so that people can hear the many different stories of student loan debt. Not everyone has the same situation.

When people aren't afraid to discuss their debt they can hopefully learn about better loan options, refinancing, and choose what's right for them.

It also lets future generations make more informed choices based on the experiences of the many who have gone before them.

There's no need for anyone to feel like they have no idea what's going on and what they should do. There is plenty of information collected in each of your individual experience. If you can share that experience it can add to the pool of student loan debt knowledge.

So one side of building a national conversation about student loan debt is information sharing.

Sharing the story of debt so people can empathize and understand what you are facing.

The other side of sharing this story is to make it viral so that it's impossible for someone not to have heard about the Repayable movement. The movement that says "Student loan debt is a problem, and we're here to solve it. We will relentlessly knock down every barrier so that we can get out from under our debt and pave the way for future generations to avoid this level of debt."

How do we share that mission? This type of sharing doesn't mean you have to talk about your personal finances. It doesn't mean you have to ask anyone else about theirs. It simply means bringing it up at every opportunity.

So when can you start talking about the repayable 1bookvs1trillion movement?

Any time education comes up.

Whenever someone talks about education especially higher education the door is open to talk about the high cost of college attendance. Discuss the NCES stats that demonstrate consistent increases in the cost of attending college (room and board plus tuition) since 1962. The NCES data shows inflation adjusted information so you're comparing apples to apples.

When anyone starts talking about Senator Bernie Sanders plan for free education.

This is an easy opportunity. These people are already focusing on the price of education. You bring up additional possible solutions, compromises, and share your pipe dreams for funding higher education.

When someone starts venting about their debt.

If someone is letting off steam about how they want to buy a house, start a family, or just have more money but feel limited by their student loan debt. This person is primed and ready to talk about student loan debt.

A word of caution that they might just be venting and not really be interested in solving the problem. But go ahead and ask them what they would want to change so their situation was better. Send them to repayable.org or let them borrow your copy of this book.

If they want to move from the complaining stage to the solving stage they'll be so glad you spoke up!

Whenever you're teaching/precepting a student or shadower interested in your profession.

I can remember it being difficult as an undergraduate student to figure out how much attending pharmacy school would cost me. Truthfully, I didn't' have a very good idea and I just went for it because it seemed like it would all work out in terms of income and debt. There's was nothing scientific about it. I just "figured" I would get paid well and that my debt wouldn't be "too bad".

It is always appropriate to talk about the cost of attending college. Talk about the price of tuition and share the frequency and percentages of tuition increases you experienced while in college. This at least gives future professionals something to start with.

You may or may not feel comfortable sharing how much interest you earned on your loans during college, how much your monthly payments are, and how much money you bring home each month.

If you *are* comfortable sharing that information you've seriously empowered this young mind to understand their future finances. Good for you. Remember, repetition and regularity create new social norms and if debt is a conversation that gets had regularly it won't feel so awkward.

Ok so I want to share the repayable message. I really believe it's possible to eliminate the burden of student loan debt for future generations and to greatly lighten it for our generation. But I just don't know what to say? Why would anyone listen to me?

* Remember your why. Why are you talking about student loan debt in the first place? You want to decrease the shame associated with it. You want to dispel misconceptions. You want to increase transparency so everyone can understand and recognize student loan debt for what it is.

* Focus on telling your story. Share your long term goals and how they're impacted by student loan debt. Maybe you're sick of renting and want to buy a house but your student loan debt financially prevents you from getting a mortgage. Maybe you could technically "afford" to buy a home but your sense

of self-preservation tells you that stacking up debt isn't a good idea so you want to repay your student loans before you take on a mortgage. Instead of buying a house you rent an apartment and get a dog.

* When you're seeking advice from someone regarding student loan debt only seek advice from someone you'd trade places with. If you don't admire their financial activities then take their advice with a giant grain of salt.

* Talking about your debt removes the barrier for someone else to talk about their own debt. When people feel comfortable asking questions about their debt they can find the information they need to accomplish their repayment goals.

* Remember that not everyone is comfortable talking about finances. Student loan debt is a pretty easy topic to talk about. Generally it didn't involve irresponsible decision making and people with student loan debt are in the majority. $1.3 trillion is a shared problem. When you talk about debt you might inspire someone else to take action on their own debt.

* If we truly want student loan debt to change I need your voice to help start a movement. I can write a book, talk to my entire social circle about it, and talk to all the students I precept but it's not a wide enough circle of influence. I need each of you to enlighten your spheres. The more voices sharing transparent stories and opening up about student loan debt the more impact. The equation for spreading the word is simple; more voices=more power=more impact.

So, are you in?

Will you stand up to your own student loan debt?

Will you fully acknowledge the total cost of your debt, know your number, and accept it?

Will you talk about the impact debt has on you?

Will you call your legislators?

Will you educate future generations?

Will you talk to your employer about repayment assistance?

Will you be relentless in the mission to make student loan debt repayable?

Come join the Repayable Movement!

You can find people and tons of helpful goodies over at repayable.org

We have social media shareables so you can make this a viral, unstoppable movement. We have FB posts, tweets, and Instagram worthy images.

We also have the scripts you need to call your legislator and the links to find their phone number and social media info.

You can find the Repayable page on Facebook where we post any upcoming Repayable events, share any important legislation in the pipeline that you need to take action on, and share the helpful or humorous wealth of the internet.

Lastly you can reach out to me directly with questions, comments, or ideas to push the movement forward. I'm @therepayable on Twitter, my YouTube Channel is Repayable, and facebook. com/1bookvs1trillion. You can also email me at jeni@ repayable.org, I work hard to respond to every email.

Design Credit

All chapter artwork was sketched by Ellaine Walker of Art by Ellaine. You can find her at https://www.facebook.com/artbyellaine/

The cover of Repayable was designed by Laura Tadt. You can find her design work at https://www.etsy.com/people/lauratadt

Bibliography

[1] National Center for Education Statistics Table 330.10. Average undergraduate tuition and fees and room and board rates charged for full-time students in degree-granting postsecondary institutions, by level and control of institution: 1963-64 through 2014-15

[2] NCES Table 330.10 Average tuition and required fees, all institutions.

[3] NCES Table 330.10 Dormitory rooms, all institutions.

[4] NCES Table 330.10 Board, all institutions.

[5] NCES Table 330.10 Cost of attendance, 4-year public institutions

[6] NCES Table 330.10 Tuition and fees, 4-year public institutions

[7]   NCES <u>Table 330.10</u> Cost of attendance, 4-year private nonprofit and for-profit institutions

[8]   NCES Table 330.10 tuition and fees, 4-year private nonprofit and for-profit institutions

[9]   "Types of Aid Subsidized and Unsubsidized Loans" *Federal Student Aid,* https://studentaid.ed.gov/sa/types/loans/subsidized-unsubsidized#how-much

[10]   "Fast Facts Tuition Costs of Colleges and Universitites" *National Center for Education Statistics,* https://nces.ed.gov/fastfacts/display.asp?id=76

[11]   "Public Service Loan Forgiveness" *Federal Student Aid,* https://studentaid.ed.gov/sa/repay-loans/forgiveness-cancellation/public-service

[12]   "Teacher Loan Forgiveness" *Federal Student Aid,* https://studentaid.ed.gov/sa/repay-loans/forgiveness-cancellation/teacher

13 Teacher Cancellation Low Income Directory
    https://www.tcli.ed.gov/CBSWebApp/tcli/
    TCLIPubSchoolSearch.jsp

14 U.S. Department of Education Office of Postsec-
    ondary Education"Teacher Shortage Areas-
    Nationwide Listing 1990-1991 through 2016-2017"
    http://www2.ed.gov/about/offices/list/ope/pol/
    tsa.pdf

15 "Income -Driven Repayment Plans for Federal
    Student Loans" *Federal Student Aid,*
    https://studentaid.ed.gov/sa/sites/default/files/
    income-driven-repayment.pdf

16 "Nurse Corps Loan Repayment Program" *Health
    Resources and Services Administration.*
    http://www.hrsa.gov/loanscholarships/
    repayment/nursing/

17 Fry, Richard. "Millennials match Baby Boomers
    as largest generation in U.S. electorate, but
    will they vote?" *Pew Research Center,* http://
    www.pewresearch.org/fact-tank/2016/05/16/

millennials-match-baby-boomers-as-largest-generation-in-u-s-electorate-but-will-they-vote/

[18] Megan Barnett, Julian E. Barnes, and Danielle Knight, "Big Money On Campus: In the Multibillion-dollar World of Student Loans, Big Lenders Are Finding New Ways to Drain Uncle Sam's Coffers," U.S. News & World Report, Oct. 19, 2003

[19] Diana J. Schemo, "Cuomo Plans to Broaden Student-Lending Inquiry," New York Times, June 7, 2007

[20] U. S. Senate Health, Education, Labor and Pensions Committee, Report on Marketing Practices in the Federal Family Education Loan Program, June 14, 2007 http://files.eric.ed.gov/fulltext/ED497127.pdf

[21] Lucca et al "Credit Supply and the Rise in College Tuition: Evidence from the Expansion in Federal Student Aid Programs" Staff Report No.

733 July 2015Revised March 2016 https://www.newyorkfed.org/medialibrary/media/research/staff_reports/sr733.pdf

[22] "Federal and State Funding of Higher Education A changing landscape" *Pew Charitable Trusts,* http://www.pewtrusts.org/en/research-and-analysis/issue-briefs/2015/06/federal-and-state-funding-of-higher-education

[23] College for All Act S. 1373, 114th Congress. (2015). https://www.congress.gov/bill/114th-congress/senate-bill/1373/all-info?resultIndex=3

[24] Student Loan Repayment Assistance Act of 2015, H.R. 1713, 114th Congress. (2015). https://www.congress.gov/bill/114th-congress/house-bill/1713/all-info

[24] Student Loan Employment Benefits Act of 2016, H.R. 5382, 114th Congress. (2016). https://www.congress.gov/bill/114th-congress/house-bill/5382/all-info

25 Higher Ed Act H.R. 6239, 114th Congress. (2016). https://www.congress.gov/bill/114th-congress/ house-bill/6239/text?q=%7B%22search%22%3A %5B%22student+loans%22%5D%7D&resultInd ex=2

26 Creating Higher Education Affordability Necessary to Compete Economically Act H.R. 5310 114th Congress. (2016). https://www. congress.gov/bill/114th-congress/house-bill/5310

About the Author

Jeni Burckart, a member of the mil-
lennial generation, is a first generation
college graduate. She is immensely
proud of her education—but she
graduated with $132,000 in student-
loan debt. She wishes someone had
been able to advise her at the begin-
ning, but she refused to be daunted, making her own
financial plan and sticking with it. Now, two years later,
she has paid off nearly $50,000 of this load, and she
wants to share her secrets of money management with
everyone!

Burckart graduated from the University of Iowa
College of Pharmacy in 2013 and now works as a
clinical pharmacist specializing in critical care and
emergency medicine. Burckart is enjoying the young
professional life in La Crosse, Wisconsin, with her
eighty-pound German shepherd mix, Link. Burckart
is the author of *Repayable* and *Millennial Maxims*.